Whale!

WHALE!

K. L. Evans

University of Minnesota Press
Minneapolis | London

Published by the University of Minnesota Press
111 Third Avenue South, Suite 290
Minneapolis, MN 55401-2520
http://www.upress.umn.edu

Library of Congress Cataloging-in-Publication Data

Evans, Kim Leilani.
    Whale! / K. L. Evans.
       p.   cm.
    Includes bibliographical references (p.   ).
    ISBN 0-8166-4316-4 (alk. paper) — ISBN 0-8166-4317-2 (Pbk. : alk. paper)
    1. Melville, Herman, 1819–1891. *Moby Dick.*   2. Psychological fiction, American—History and criticism.   3. Sea stories, American—History and criticism.   4. Whaling in literature.   5. Whales in literature.   I. Title.
    PS2384.M62E93 2003
    813'.3—dc21
2003007957

Printed in the United States of America on acid-free paper

The University of Minnesota is an equal-opportunity educator and employer.

12 11 10 09 08 07 06 05 04 03   10 9 8 7 6 5 4 3 2 1

For Professor Ken Dauber,
in token of my admiration

CONTENTS

PREFACE

I HAD AN ODD BEDFELLOW ONCE, a Melville scholar (or sculler, she liked to say). I was in the Antipodes, chasing ice. When the weather didn't turn me back I hitched rides on a Hercules Transport out of New Zealand—cavernous, no seats, mesh webbing to strap oneself into—down to Beardmore Glacier, Antarctica. Oxford had recently accepted my doctorate on glaciology, but most people found the occupation amusing. Not the Melville scholar, though. She kept asking me about friction, and the blinding white, and how to read snow. Her questions crabbed sideways: often my explanations seemed to turn up some scuttling fancy, so that she provisioned herself with material I didn't quite believe but had somehow myself supplied. She was a queer fish among critics; her curiosity was all for ideas. Someone gave me a bookmark once with a quote from Coleridge on it: "I regard truth as a divine ventriloquist: I care not from whose mouth the sounds are supposed to proceed." Her connections smelled of inaccuracy and invention, but they were pleasing—they pleased me and so provided their own legitimacy. This immodest manner of measurement reminded me of how temperature at the Pole could drop down and pass beyond the weather. Who's to say what cold is.

I made her laugh by asking, after she read me the first few pages of her book on *Moby Dick,* "I like it. But are you allowed to put in all those fishy witticisms?" She said she hoped so. A poet I know has said in passing that scientists can seem like embarrassing, marginal figures (almost like poets) in the new corporate world. I think this is because whatever it is we do seems either to have no words or to require all of them, all the words. When I got the notice—down at the Amundsen-Scott South Pole Station, the envelope white and cold like everything else—that the Melville scholar had named me as the person she wished to provide a preface to her book, I was taken aback. I had left her puttering around New Zealand, reading old whalers' logs and dreaming about ships. Then I realized that we are probably in the same business, slipping around on uncertain surfaces and giving readings of what look to most people like paintings of white figures on white backgrounds. (There is nothing like the Antarctic for furnishing lessons on the glaring incongruities of sameness.) Have we made up some of the borders and edges? Most certainly. Has that stopped us from negotiating some kind of useful account?

January 12, 2003
Scott Base, Antarctica

PREAMBLE

ONE QUESTION UNDERLIES ALL OF *MOBY DICK:* "So what's eating you?" Many readers of the novel have put this question to its author, coming up with pat explanations of what is called Melville's pessimism, or madness—even genius—as a response to his father's breakdown or his poverty or his sexuality or his marriage, instead of asking the question of themselves, which is really what should be asked, and is asked, by Melville, and not rhetorically, What is eating *us,* what is eating *you?*

The whaling business is not a safe one. One of the inspirations for Melville's narrative is the story of the Nantucket rig *Essex,* stove in and sunk by a whale. To a nineteenth-century audience, increasingly sure of its mastery over the natural world, it was an extraordinary idea that the monster could turn on its persecutors and deliberately sink not just a whaleboat but the mother ship. "Whale sinks whaler" is your ultimate man-bites-dog story, but not because it implies a simple reversal of fortunes. If in hot pursuit of dinner one is oneself targeted by another's appetite, then the game has changed. Whale sinks whaler invites the suggestion that there is no safe place from which to begin a critique. No outside, no dry platform, no guest's visiting privilege. A confident distinction between hunter and prey dissolves into an individual's irreversible entanglement in the nature of things.

The lesson of whale hunting is that the creature, not to be found on land, is caught at a certain cost: the whaler must get wet. The whaler must get lost, or at least lose his sense of immunity, which never survives the sea. In *Moby Dick* whaling is less a vocation than a way of looking at the world from a position inside it. Thus what its author calls for from his readers is not commentary so much as tenacity, answerability, affection. This is a novel that begins not like a book but, with its opening line, like a relationship. Ishmael introduces himself in such a way—suicidal without repentance but somehow solicitous for commiseration—that a reader must wonder what kind of person he is. Which occasions concern, presuming one engages the offer of company, about what kind of person oneself is, or will prove to be, when the ship begins to leak while lowering for whales in a gale off Cape Horn. (When the ship hits the fan.)

What *Moby Dick* asks for, or calls for, is a different kind of investigation, one that should more properly be called philosophical. Writing is philosophical when its author's self-inspection occasions an assault on his assumptions—an introspection that usually forces the confession that absolute and certain foundations for epistemological claims are elusive. Melville calls this unmooring *getting to sea*. But if, after losing sight of the land, investigating foundations turns to investigating the grounds of psychology, an examination of the world is displaced by an examination of one's position in regard to the world. Once come undone, in other words, an individual can begin to wonder where, and how, to locate himself. Discover to what he owes obedience, and with whom he is in community. Melville calls this joint venture *quietly taking to ship*. Of course, once launched in the direction of self-discovery, it is always possible to flounder. What if you can't find yourself? What if you are looking in the wrong places?

It would appear that the opposite of certainty is skepticism, or that feeling oneself lost is equal to feeling the world lost, or out of reach. But that these things—feeling lost, and feeling the world lost—are in *Moby Dick* not at all equivalent seems to me a fact worth reporting. Finding the world lost is the skeptical conclusion, and it warrants an individual's withdrawal from worldly responsibilities. Finding oneself lost simply suggests the necessity of asking where one's confidences lie, or where they can rest and where they incriminate themselves. Finding oneself lost begs the question of investment; it means venturing a shared interest in the world's securities in anticipation of being able to go on in a certain way.

An appropriate response to *Moby Dick*, in light of its philosophical disposition, is not to lay open a character like Captain Ahab, or try to understand his motives as if one were in his shoe. The intense emotion that drives Ahab is not to be rationalized, but attended to.

One mustn't track him but test his leads by treating the expression of his desire as that which directs readerly attention to the site of commotion—to the whale. This *public* aspect of the whale is the concern of *Moby Dick*. Because Ahab must not only find himself by locating his whale, he must show that he can do this companionably, or at least not alone: his whale can't be taken seriously unless it is recognized by an assembly. Another way of putting this is to say that there is no means by which Ahab can claim his right to the whale as part of an overall right to privacy. His belief requires endorsement because for him believing is inherently a public project. Once readers are clear that they, too, should look in the direction of the whale, they can abandon the traffic in explication and put their minds to investigating what manner of creature they imagine themselves.

At sea there is no possibility of assimilation along amphibian lines. A person who has lost the ground beneath his feet cannot pretend to be a fish and swim to safety. How, then, is inept man to cross this sea and secure his supper? (His livelihood, his liberty, his composure?) Timely sacrifice seems the most popular defense against hostile seas and impossible journeys. That old, curious daring of responding to the terrors of implication by jumping overboard, quietly wishing for a tightly caulked, tranquil-fishy belly of a place one can willingly Jonah oneself into. Or in the language of the academy, an acceptance of the inevitable and extinguishing gulf between the subject and his world—a Derridean assurance that one's sense of direction, or ability to determine what things mean, is only ever a construction in an endlessly regressive process of signification.

This acquiescing shrug, this leap (of theorists and felons before God), gestures toward saying that because everything touches me, nothing can touch me, or be asked of me, because I am lost, as it were, to myself. Philosophically this trade consists of survival by assimilation, a resistance based on resignation that amounts to giving oneself over to the world's operations by accepting and enduring them. It might be called the modern temper—the hope of a certain security along the lines of total capitulation. A kind of preservation or safe location in the bowels of the world that is achieved by hurling oneself into its deepest belly.

But the whaling industry rejects this digestive model. A man who thinks he belongs at sea—that somehow he can become a natural part of its operations—is marked as a landlubber. Oceans do not forgive the feigned nonchalance of a tourist who acts like a local. So the surprise that comes with big-game fishing—the sudden realization that what you've got has really gotten you—must accompany the whaler-savvy that getting in with the creature you came to slay is a veritable impossibility. The postmodern suggestion is to survive drowning by becoming a thing impervious to layered depths, admitting yourself touched on all sides and so somehow an animal of the ocean. The whaling industry finds this solution shoddy. *Of course* one is in the water: but to make like a fish is the stuff of comedy or tragedy. Better to make out the fish, make it to the fish, which is a whaler's sense that the point is not to survive the ocean's depths but to negotiate its conditions.

The industry's first lesson is that to know what a whale means (and thus what the word *whale* means) is commensurate with being prepared for some of its uses. Whaling's risk is that its slippery prize may never be brought home; but its slippery prize, to those for whom such battles are worth fighting, is the recovery of the writerly conceit of saying something meaningful, or the readerly conceit of saying that something has meaning. The point of describing the real and imagined use of whales is to loosen the hold of the confused way of looking at language that is the product of the philosopher's impoverished diet of examples. Such a diet suggests there are, at best, only two ways of using words: using them as if we didn't mean them or using them in meaningless ways. In hopes of showing how absurd it is to expect language use to conform to these narrow possibilities, the subject of this book is a collection of evidence that supports other ways of thinking about the meanings of words.

Words are not private, but public. (Or even though its possibility is astonishing, I can say something to you, and you can know what I mean.) Following Wittgenstein, following Melville, this text is an attempt to construct a model for competently capturing a shared term. But because I don't want to be left with an imaginary object at the center of my analysis, I will, following Ahab, use the term *whale*.

{ 1 }
A Tale of Attachment

Philosophy is a leaky boat which must
be repaired while at sea.
—*Wittgenstein,* Philosophical Investigations

Sail Ho!
—*Ahab, in* Moby Dick

IF WHAT FEELS LIKE the willful destruction in *Moby Dick* is
a sign not of the ruin of despair but of a kind of vandalism of
that ruin—or if the violence of this story forsakes an original
violence for commentary, the way graffiti defaces an already
demolished edifice—then what feels like destruction may simply
be a refusal to turn away from the wreck, a gesture that directs
the attention of passersby to injury that should not be viewed
with accustomed indifference but examined, as if for clues as to
its cause. If we are talking about vandalism, and not destruction, of the kind that requires you to look nowhere else than to
what is happening, it seems obvious that there must be some
other violence, against which the events of *Moby Dick* react,
near enough and familiar enough to the neighborhood of this
novel's writer that the threatened territory calls for marking.
Defacement of the artistic variety speaks out of two mouths,
at once asking for help and attention even while promising
that the noted wrecks are spoken for, are covered, are under
control. If the injury to which *Moby Dick* furiously addresses itself is a public matter (as only a public matter would prompt a

communal address), it suggests that what drives the novel is not a private hurt but some more common or shared grievance. Private hurts inspire world-consuming revenge, but public hurts call for something else, more readily in the vicinity of repair, or restoration. What instigates public objection is the sense that valuable things are under threat, or that the idea of what is valuable is getting lost. The violence is a sign of the search for the valuable. In these cases the hunt for the missing thing, which may be not so much missing as hard to determine, or hard to find, is powered not by malevolence—but by love.

To suggest that *Moby Dick* is a tale not of vengeance but of affection does not compromise its reputation as action-adventure. This is because the manner in which it chooses to express its tenderness is indeed in the form of an attack. But what is attacked is philosophy's wish to prove beyond reasonable doubt the existence of a gulf separating fact (or the existence of things) from value (or the freedom to determine the meaning of those things). What is attacked is the insistence that the capacity to know what things mean is absent or unavailable, and that this unavailability is the cause for skepticism. What is attacked is the skeptical conclusion, the worldly resignation that knowledge's demands are too big, too exhausting, to survive. The object of Ahab's tireless assault is to rescue from skeptical demise a world not despairing of itself, or not threatened by the *impossibility* of knowing how to determine the meaning of its objects and events. Thus *Moby Dick* is a tale of attachment, disguised as vengeance, about the search for connection, camouflaged to resemble estrangement. Under love's license this story risks impertinent questions about the nature of involvement, particularly whether philosophy is right to assume that the experience of being in the world—implicated, fouled, in the thick of things—is what gets in the way of knowledge, and not what makes it possible.

To be clear, when I say something like "whether philosophy is right," I refer to the practice whose aim is to ensure a person can distinguish something being so from her *wanting* or *believing* it to be so, and philosophy most often stakes its claim to this knowledge on the basis of a systematic limitation of reason's powers. But if distinguishing fact from value is philosophy's responsibility, the burden and curse of this task is also its peculiar preoccupation, as surely as the white whale is Ahab's peculiar preoccupation.

Like divorce, philosophy involves machinery that eases conflict but also acts in its interest. Philosophy of mind, for instance, has been so captivated by the axiom that we ought to know what we are doing that it has, and not without chagrin, taken great pains to isolate the self from reason, appetite, and belief. But seeing as reason, appetite, and belief make up so much of what is going on, the world of the self has grown small next to *what we call* the world of the self. Facts are dwarfed by thought, which grabs for itself the bulk of existence. The brain is wider than the sky, Emily Dickinson says. The brain is deeper than the sea.

But even as tiny fact is overwhelmed by thought, it is *thought* that, unless directed toward an active conclusion, is considered cloudy and indefinite. If mental life is indeed a shadow of public life, or life in the sun, it follows that the life of the mind must be mooching off the outer life, the life potentially open to different observers. Subsequently the inner life, hidden from view, depends for analysis on overt moments of public activity; thought cannot be judged until it has become action—until it has, as it were, broken the surface. But these are considerable assumptions. Especially when it will be seen that in accordance with them the inner life or life of the mind cannot be included within the interpretable, moral domain.

If what goes on inwardly is hidden from us, then appraisal and judgment can extend just to the publicly observable and be concerned only with public acts. If philosophy is right when it says that we can have no knowledge of the interior, then as regards ethical considerations the life of the mind is to all intents and purposes both meaningless and irrelevant. If inner data are incommunicable and uninterpretable, their evaluation is a strange and incomprehensible exercise. Mental states, according to this view, do not deserve interpretation. Or if an interpretation is offered, it is either entirely arbitrary or the result of a privileged position, an insider's track (knowledge of one's own mind, say).

Is it impossible to give a reading of the inner workings of a thing that is not yourself? If the answer is yes, then "interpretation" must deal only with clear and distinct movements. What is called reading would simply be the process of following overt actions, and the job of readers would be to record these instances of movement. The procedure (the allusion is Henri Bergson's) would be akin to marking only the physical operations of actors on a set. Actors' movements, and not their intentions, would determine the significance of the performance; thus pantomime, slapstick, and all histrionic art would be more meaningful than the delicate drama or comedy, of which one could say little.

That mental states cannot be interpreted poses an interesting problem for ethics, too. Unable to frame or assign action, only record it, the ethical is reduced to a series of pronouncements after the fact: such-and-such action is good or bad. Moral concepts, like tourists on a beach, may marvel at the landscape but they do not determine it. But moral concepts, as Iris Murdoch says, "do not move about *within* a hard world set up by science and logic. They set up, for different purposes, a different world." That morality does indeed encompass the life of the mind is her point. What we call "ethics" is not an account of what we regard in such a way, but the manner and form in which the regard is mounted. Quite unlike a system of classification, ethics is the *condition* that indicates a quality of circumstance.

To keep ethics from being turned from a state of being into a kind of verdict, value judgments must be allowed to infiltrate the grand jurisdiction of thought. Only by giving reading back its absolute authority, or allowing it access to what goes on inwardly, is it possible to rescue from incomprehensibility the interpretable object. This, of course, is what Ahab is attempting to do. What is strange and counterintuitive about *Moby Dick* is that any inclination to accompany Ahab on his quest (of rescuing the interpretable object) feels like abandoning the moral universe. When in fact—well, when in fact the case is entirely otherwise.

Where does this story begin? Or rather, what is the manner of its approach? Certainly *Moby Dick* is quick to confess its vernacular, idiomatic quality—the fact that it has a perspective, a preference, an address—which binds it to that school of thought for which such a disclosure inaugurates, rather than concludes, what is called philosophy. Because ever since cognition could be shown to be inseparable from the contingencies of fact, knowledge of the world ceased to be the kind of thing that one could approach gracefully, like an angel, and not gauchely, like one's tedious self. Maybe the first to intuit philosophy's pedestrian quality, Descartes still hoped to evade this human sentence by conducting his thoughts "in such an order that, by commencing with objects the simplest and easiest to know, I might ascend by little and little, and, as it were, step by step, to the knowledge of the more complex." His goal was to approach an idea from its careful edges, so that his own trace and scent need not scare off the truth of it. Accordingly Cartesian method—like gently gently catching monkeys—champions the idea that a concept may be advanced upon by degrees.

These careful stagings include the intelligence that the inner workings of an individual's mind give meaning to her thoughts and that these meanings are captured, in some sense, by language. Here ideas are accessible *through* language, and language is learned in a fairly straightforward manner. Augustine had explained this model of language acquisition: "When they (my elders) named some object, and accordingly moved towards something, I saw this and I grasped that the thing was called by the sound they uttered when they meant to point it out. . . . Thus, as I heard words repeatedly used in their proper places in various sentences, I gradually learnt to understand what objects they signified; and after I had trained my mouth to form these signs, I used them to express my own desires." Augustine describes the use of language to get to ideas, the way that I might use my car to get to the supermarket. I might not reach the one without the other, but they are by no means the same. (In contrast, modern philosophy understands language as not merely a vehicle for thought but itself practical consciousness; language does not just express thought but directs it. Because it is impossible to think outside of language, it is also impossible to language outside of practice—or make words mean apart from their use.)

What is especially odd about Augustine's explanation of how language works, though, is his contention that one "gradually" learns a language in a general sense, but in the particular one must "grasp" (an action indicating haste as well as agility) "that the thing was called by the sound . . . uttered." It is potentially the problem of *grasping* what a thing means, of what grasping amounts to, that troubled Descartes and forced him to acknowledge the possibility of *things not adding up*—to recognize skepticism, in other words, as a plausible adversary. If doing philosophy means using language, and learning what things mean seems to employ two conflicting strategies, the one rash and headlong, the other circumspect and accumulative, then philosophy appears to require a kind of mindful solicitation in its handling. This carefulness, shyly evident in the writing of the *Meditations,* is less like exactness than discretion. It stems from a creeping worry, a spreading damp under the foundations of thought that leads to the sense that the ground beneath one's feet is buckling, or cracking up, or, at least, calling for special attention—as if movement is necessary but there are eggshells everywhere underfoot.

But if doubt is what marks Descartes's text for modernity, it is his refusal to genuinely engage these worries that make his writing sound gimmicky. Passingly sensitive to what Emerson later calls the "lubricity" of the human condition, or the quality of material description that makes things slide away from us when we reach to describe them, Descartes endearingly picks something sticky—wax—as his favored philosophical object. And though he claims induction as a method, or careful step-by-step reasoning, his arguments often spurt across the finish line. The funny thing about his *cogito,* to a new reader, is that incongruous *ergo,* the "therefore," which does all its work in private, in the back room. Reading Descartes's *Meditations* gives one the sense of having witnessed a drug bust; bang down the door on the left, and one meets with a speechless quick chaotic bundling of substance. At the crucial moment of explanation he swallows or flushes: scuffle scuffle, *therefore* knowledge! *Therefore* God! Ultimately Descartes suppresses the anxiety he feels about the human capacity to know—but it is his caution, his sense that philosophy requires a kind of vigilance, that marks the discipline as one haunted by skepticism.

Classical philosophy makes a distinction between language and thought. But if there is a difference between words and meaning, or if they come together but are not the same, how does one cross this distance? If I learn the word "table" because you point to a table and say the word, how do I learn the word "because"? Some words, when we grasp at them, slip through our fingers. Modern philosophy says there is no distinction between language and thought. A word gets its meaning from the way it is used and not from its direct relation to an object. Under the new order language is emancipated from the close quarters under which Augustine had it confined. Language can have life, so that my attention is not limited to what something *is* but may discover the more interesting matter of what I might do with it.

However, I am now faced with new, seemingly insurmountable difficulties; if words aren't directly attached to things, how do users of a common language know what words mean? How do you know to which table I am referring, if I cannot or choose not to point to it? How do you determine, if I ask you to bring me the large table, and I point out the one I want, "tableness" from "largeness"—why is it that you can never bring me the "large"? Or if the table looks large to me, and small to you (because you have a bigger one at home), how is it that we both know what we are talking about? How do different speakers share the same words?

Experience leads to the truth of competing perspectives, which suggests that an individual's understanding of the world is unique. Knowledge is constructed out of experience, and every individual's experience is different—this much is certain. But declaring the sovereignty of difference or uniqueness is also the skeptic's peculiar brand of despotism. If we use the same words to describe differing experience, does that mean that the words somehow fail us? Or that they don't do what we think they do? Or if they do manage to work in this way, how is it that all this work seems to get done in the back room, out of sight? We know words work but we can't seem to figure out how. This poetic perplexity puts strain on thought's affections, leaving philosophers feeling as if they married the language of strangers.

Since claims to the real sound increasingly hollow as soon as perception is admitted to be relative, which is what experience teaches, a diplomatic response is to try to save the real world by unchaining the truth of things from our knowledge of them. (The idea being that as long as man thinks his knowledge is not real unless it conforms to real things, it follows he can never know anything at all.) Perhaps it is unnecessary that nature or the material of the world come under suspicion, just because the means of knowing it are suspect. What must be investigated, then, are not facts but determinations. Where does a thing end and man's understanding of it begin? This is the empirical project. But empiricism has the added effect of exposing as fraudulent philosophy that hopes to approach thought from the careful edges. Man does not live on the world, but in it, and the material of his philosophy, like the bulk of his person, is subject to the laws of matter.

Locke, for example, wonders that if liberty "is the power to act or not act, according as the mind directs," when does this liberty happen? Is it suspended, somehow, *after* the judgment of the understanding and *before* determination of the will? A good scientist, Locke argues that the supposed philosophical ability to suspend judgment, what other philosophers called "indifferency," is a fantasy. If liberty, or choice, is made possible by that indifferent or suspended moment between understanding and determining, how is this moment conceivable, or what kind of being is capable of it? As Locke says, "the determination of the will immediately follows the judgment of the understanding: and to place liberty at an indifferency, antecedent to the thought and judgment of the understanding, seems to me to place liberty in a state of darkness, wherein we can neither see nor say anything of it."

Locke is here investigating the meaning of terms like "before" and "after" as applied to discernment—because if philosophers think they can break the process of comprehension into distinguishable pieces, then they know nothing about matter. When he says that the determination of the will "immediately follows" the judgment of the understanding, he is not asking his readers to imagine the kind of following that is familiar from a line of elephants, or sheep, where one trips on the heels of another. His rejection of the term "indifferent" in favor of "immediate" is meant to indicate that the body of man is substance always in the gradual process of construction, and there is no point at which he is clearly not one thing and not yet another, not understanding and not determining, not twenty-nine and not thirty. To pretend that man or his mind is somehow outside of or above the laws of matter is to place that supposed liberty "in a state of darkness," which is one way of saying to take away all access to it.

To presume agency without the agent is to play at philosophy as if from a safe distance. Locke's "immediately follows" supposes association as that which comes during, inside of, a relationship. It cannot be entered into cautiously. Better to think of association as the way someone enters water. There is never any point at which one is in the water but not yet wet. Water cannot be entered by degrees. (Though you may put your toe in but not your torso, what is meant by "in" has not changed.) Locke's practice diverges from a Cartesian one on this crucial point: it disallows preparatory movements toward philosophy. His puzzled investigation of liberty has the effect of sounding like someone who is beginning to study philosophy and somehow already has its idea on his mind.

Kantian efforts, in light of these difficulties, hoped to preserve a realm of moral freedom independent from the contingencies of fact. The most violent part of this project is a wish to secure the validity of cognitive claims by establishing their independence from the will and desire—to wrest from the world a distinction between "fact" and "value." Philosophy is this struggle. But it is also, under the name of aesthetics, a *response* to this separation. If philosophy indicates the gulf between being and wanting, it is also a reflection on that impossible division and distance, an abashed investigation of what is lost or what goes missing as a result of the dissolution.

Doubt is what sends philosophy looking for foundations. But what happens to philosophy when it goes looking for this solid ground? It finds that knowledge is not built on a natural or given base but constructed, as it were, on the open ocean of experience. Thus epistemological claims remain vulnerable to allegations about their standing. The loss of foundations means that human knowledge lacks a certain security, which is like saying that philosophers must operate, not from land, but from sea: "Like sailors who must rebuild their ship on the open sea," Otto Neurath says, "never able to dismantle it in dry-dock and reconstruct it there out of the best materials." Philosophy's convictions must be portable and contingent: "And when we cease our attempt to drive our piles into a deeper layer," Karl Popper says of these temporary dwellings, "it is not because we have reached firm ground. We simply stop when we are satisfied that they are firm enough to carry the structure, at least for the time being."

In this vein, though, philosophers suffer grave disappointment. The nearest one can come to knowing is to analyze knowledge and so grasp which techniques are available for understanding the world. But if the grounds for a critique are drawn from experience, they are susceptible to motives of affinity and preoccupation—the subject is always herself subject to her world. If the ship stands for the subject or language or thought and it must rely on itself for repair, this sets up for philosophy a particular kind of problem, perhaps best articulated by Wittgenstein's promise that "philosophy is a leaky boat which must be repaired while at sea." The problem is that the material of philosophy's rescue is also the material of its grief; the boat's leak is the relentless reminder that the business of conceptualizing the world is affected by the fact of being in it.

Thought's inability to waterproof itself, or be certain of its operations, causes some philosophers concern—it being hard to shake the feeling that if it leaks, there must be something wrong with it. Somberly, philosophy survives the impossible through exacting self-consciousness, using as the material of connection its own confessed sadness at the inexorable distance between itself and the world. It forges ahead with confidence, but it is a conviction based on dissatisfaction, even awed dissatisfaction at its own success. What happens to philosophy that investigates foundations is that it encounters the probability that there is no such thing as certainty in matters epistemic. Man is a bachelor frigate—gifted with an affinity for adventure, but entirely, terrifyingly unattached. This does not mean that philosophy's goals are profitless, but that its securities are impermanent. Meaning may be looked for, but philosophy assures us that what satisfaction can be had is in meaning's chase, not its capture. After a point we choose to come to a rest because we have to, because we grow tired.

In a streak of inspired melancholia the analytic tradition, or that practice sprung from the custom of establishing which conditions license relevant claims, did not eradicate skepticism but made possible its institutionalization. The tradition satisfied its own expectations by *acceding* to its limits—it found its voice by investigating the confines within which it could speak. In fact the concluding words of the *Tractatus Logico-Philosophicus,* for which Ludwig Wittgenstein first grew famous, were these:

"What we cannot speak about we must pass over in silence." The *Tractatus* had primarily been concerned with clarifying what were the limits of language—its object to demonstrate how cramped the area of reasonable talk really was. Upon finding that the best philosophy could do was talk about itself, Wittgenstein seemed to recommend that philosophy had nothing more to say.

This reticence was due in part to the fact that the discipline had grown under an ethos that largely accepted the isolation of a recognizable malfunction as an appropriate system for studying and trying to correct it. The distinguishing feature of work that recognized what kinds of utterances could be considered meaningful was the vigor with which it pointed out the necessity of examining the scope and bounds of significant discourse. But the habit of this scrutiny was to quarantine meaning in order to better inspect it, and the closer philosophers looked, the less there was to see. They were left wondering what, if anything, connects language to the world.

The most exciting contribution of the analytic tradition is the basic idea that the nature of concepts is not fixed independently from the concepts that correspond to them. Members of this school propose that humans should picture themselves not as detached observers of the world but as objects moving about in constant relation to other objects. But the tradition's most troublesome aspect is its harmless-sounding proposition that all objects are distinguished from each other on a comparative basis. *Comparison* (one knows a white whale because it is not a red whale, or dead whale, or dreadful wail) suggests that recognition of a thing depends on its relationship to other things, which sounds perfectly reasonable until one remembers this pattern of recognition still understands identification of a thing as that which happens *after* it has been seen but *before* it has been judged or assimilated into a meaningful system. Along these lines an object's meaning may be understood as a result of its classification. Meaning is in a sense given to the object after it has been apprehended, as if interpretation of a thing is something we may or may not indulge in, at various levels of the game. And here is the catch: because this approach assumes it is possible to decide to *begin* looking for the meaning of a thing, it also suggests it is a matter of decision, of convention, where to stop looking for the meaning of a thing. If one can stop looking for meaning, it is only a matter of time until one does stop. This too is the threat of skepticism.

What is important to understand about skepticism is that it is the result not of having too few options but of having too many. In effect, skepticism is a disaster area of intention. The trenches of World War I (in which Wittgenstein puzzled out much of the writing of the *Tractatus*) are a prime illustration of how one can come to feel cramped, or otherwise stifled, because of too much opportunity. The stalemate of the trenches is a venture, like skepticism, of giving up *because* one can go on and on. The analytic tradition hopes to tame the vastness, the almost limitless prospect, it discovers under its feet (after looking for foundations and finding them absent) by narrowing down its margin of possibility. But instead of fighting off skepticism, the strategy ensures it. As Wittgenstein shows convincingly in the *Tractatus,* any attempt to restrict the bounds of discourse ends up not freeing the word but making its practical use impossible—which means that all philosophy has left to talk about is its own improbability.

Although this stance suggests the likelihood of becoming more and more tight-lipped, those who wish to be undefeated by skepticism must find a way to make response inevitable. They must show how it is possible to use words—not just the easy proper names but normative-descriptive adjectives, shifty and featureless articles, vague pronouns—and to use them like they mean them. They must show that knowing what a word means cannot entail the difficulty of remembering, or calling up as if from careful study, a word's definition, but instead demands its immediate recognition. They must show how the meaning of a word does not accompany it, as if there were a choice to the matter, as if one may use a word but decline its meaning, or have it on the side, or save it for later. (If Ahab has something to contribute to the battle against skepticism, it is this: *meaning comes at us*—aye, whether we provoke it or not. There is no recognition of a thing without recognition of its meaning. Meaningfulness is not an amenity, but a requirement.)

Those who do not wish to succumb to skepticism must show that knowing what a thing means is the condition on which recognition of it stands. What must be adopted, as far as philosophy goes, is a much more expansive kind of investigation. Something, perhaps, along the lines of what occurred to Wittgenstein after the war—the kind of search that impels one, as he remarks in the preface to *Philosophical Investigations*, "to travel over a wide field of thought criss-cross in every direction." When quarantine and silence proved an imperfect resistance, he returned to his old interests with a renewed sense of the commotion still befitting his profession. What happened to Wittgenstein was that he began to wonder in how *large* an area one might look for what one wanted to find. In his early work an interest in the particular, entangled movements of language had been dug out from narrow troughs: in his later work he brings this same fascination with the vernacular landscape to the grandest sweep he can imagine. He reconfigures his investigation in more ample environs, never abandoning his early interest in the local and particular but swelling and vastly multiplying the circumference of his study.

Wittgenstein's revision of the philosopher's quest politely sends Odysseus back to his boat. He rewrites the voyager's homecoming to accommodate the space that language philosophy needs—returning his hero again and again to the open sea. (His hero, of course, is philosophy, which finds peace when it no longer needs to bring *itself* into question.) The land appears welcome to men who are swimming, "after Poseidon has smashed their strong-built ship on the open / water, pounding it with the weight of wind and the heavy / sea." But landed with language, these shore-bound men are no further from their leaky boats. They would happily anchor, but the anchorage is quagmire, and there is nothing quite as useless as a boat stranded in the mud. At sea, though, a leaky boat has a chance.

Is it unreasonable for a philosopher to speak of chance? Does it make his work unscientific—or in other words does the acceptance of chance (as hope) bar from philosophy claims to the serious that the rejection of chance (as luck, or wishful thinking) ensures for it? Has philosophy somehow struck a devil's deal with skepticism, so that what is given the name "philosophy" is that which invests in skepticism as a certainty, while that which entertains skepticism as a *possibility* is given some other less scientific title, namely, literature? However, it is with chance, sometimes called coincidence, that science has most often had to occupy itself—investigating, for instance, how the world seems to hold itself together, how it keeps from falling apart. How in the course of evolution have there been so many improbable odds? This has always been a problem for biologists, who must wonder how myriad accidents and mutations come together with the consonance of a mechanism such as the eye, so that the thing seems both foreseen and contingent. It is also a problem for language users, who know that if you are smart, words can't really be trusted to take you where you want them to—but if you are effective, they seem to manage it anyway. On the subject of chance, Nicholas Mosley, the author of *Hopeful Monsters,* has a character declare: "There should be some Noah's Ark in the mind, if there are to be held the results of all these almost unimaginable coincidences." How does one hold the results of coincidence? Would such a container ever be waterproof?

If corralling coincidences together long enough to find a pattern depends on an act of recognition, or collection, it almost seems as if one has to accomplish this feat without meaning to. Like the American constitutional promise to "hold these truths as self-evident," the act depends on the manual equivalent of a sidelong glance—an agreement to agree on terms that don't agree, a "self-evidence" that needs to be held as such. This kind of holding is less like grasping than attracting, and only when we are at our most attractive do we stand a chance of amassing the necessary congregation. The most "unhandsome" part of the human condition, Emerson says, is this "evanescence and lubricity of all objects, which lets them slip through our fingers then when we clutch hardest." To build the ship that survives the unnavigable sea that washes silent waves between us and all things we aim at and converse with is to erect a particular kind of boat, one that does not try to escape the ocean so much as employ it. An Ark in the mind anchors itself in provisional constructions and not natural facts, which means it does not attempt to land but finds a certain support in the open erudition of the sea. Accordingly she must be constructed under the laws of attraction, not causality. Subject to whim and accident, she leaks. But does this mean she is in need of repair?

The project of *Philosophical Investigations* turns away from seeing the condition of being at sea in a leaky boat as tragedy. That our craft mixes with the element of its support is simply proof that we and the universe are a mutually creating organism. In place of the old fear of drowning is the suggestion that we are going about philosophy in the wrong way, trying to get ourselves onto dry land, or even into a dry boat, when in fact the ocean offers its own kind of protection, and not because we are one of its creatures. One could say that what opens up Wittgenstein's later work is his sense that the promise of philosophy's condition is that the means of its grief—language—is also the means of its rescue. I understand *Philosophical Investigations* to be a mariner's manual: taking the leaky boat of language as its subject, it explains how we *think* the boat leaks because it is badly built or somehow lacks the tools necessary for repair, but in fact the boat leaks because it is a boat, and the seeping intrusion of our surroundings does not get in the way of our navigation but makes navigation possible.

By placing more trust in the ocean—a system of support that Wittgenstein comes to call "grammar"—he takes pressure off the need to fix his boat. His modified station dislodges him from the ranks of the sailor school of philosophy (or that anti-foundationalist tradition which intuits that because the foundations are missing, the subject is at sea) and enlists him in its smelly, less legitimate counterpart, the whale fishery. For a sailor, the ocean is an adversary one must resist in order to complete one's job; but a whaler's particular business is to use the ocean, not cross it, searching its vastness for profit. Merchant sailors could finish a voyage without much more than a glance over the taffrail, while whalers were forced by their profession into regular contemplation of the vast blue basin in which they found themselves. Unlike the sailor school the whale fishery invests its interests in the sea, not the boat. And an ordinary language philosopher like Wittgenstein comes to look for words the way a whaler looks for whales.

The bulk of this particular work looks at Wittgenstein's investigation of the new watery region in the context of a whaler's story. The best tale of leaky boats I know is the one told by Melville, in light of his own decision to explore large territory. I am suggesting that a whaler's account of how to look for whales (a model based not on recognition but on employment) is the clearest illustration of Wittgenstein's contention that using language is not a tragic-comic grope from the deep end toward the shallow but a certain, meditated turning toward the open ocean, *an ocean that provides support.* That the support is conditional, that it demands a kind of calculated effort, a constant treading of water, does not render it valueless. This is because the opposite of skepticism is not certainty but commitment—even preoccupation.

Philosophy that only works by calling itself into question always carries the possibility of refusing its own solicitation, of succumbing to skepticism or becoming unresponsive. But if philosophy replaces the search for foundations with the search for something else, something closer to home, is philosophical fatigue less likely? The beauty of looking for something else, *anything* else, besides foundations, is that one is bound to encounter the home truth that whatever is discovered is inescapably subject to one's own view of it. An investigation of that thing will only ever produce a compendium of the investigator. Which means that no matter what it chooses, so long as it chooses something, philosophy replaces the search for foundations with the search for finding oneself.

In this approach it is necessary not to look out onto the thing as if through a preexisting subjectivity but to acknowledge the thing as part of yourself, by finding whoever you may be by virtue of your bearing in the world. Subjective prejudice, in other words, is not what keeps the world at a distance but what ensures its nearness. That is to say, the circumstances of finding oneself entail finding the world, or finding oneself connected to it in ways impossible to disengage from or grow weary of. Finding oneself, which is the making of such an ordinary, familiar search, battles the agoraphobia that comes with looking for what holds the world together. It is a situation that calls for special attention or maintenance, but not despair. Its only requirement is a kind of self-reliance—that you come to terms with your own unsettled and unsettling qualities. That you keep it together, or not fall apart, even as you find yourself in pieces, or part of something too large to contemplate.

Philosophy that replaces the search for foundations with the search for finding oneself is where *Moby Dick* commences. It should be remembered, too, that although the quest appears to be embarked upon with a certain eagerness it is an involuntary zeal. Philosophy that discovers this kind of connection to the world begins at the hand of unwelcome intrusion; these are musings sprung from painful contradictions. They are the demands of one's necessary employment, not speculative academic adventure. In the chapters that follow I look at Ahab's constant, indescribable, almost lunatic state of agitation as indicative of a philosophy determined to neither ignore the threat of skepticism nor become prostrate in the face of it—philosophy that rides out the possibility of skepticism, or disconnection to the world, by cunningly anchoring itself in the self. This reading understands Ahab's search for the whale to be undertaken at a moment of crisis and pursued with the conviction that the source of the crisis is himself—but also that in undertaking the search for himself, Ahab is attempting not to reject or abandon the world but to save it. An investigation of this search will have far-reaching results, since upon the question of *what goes on inwardly* (the veiled and clandestine process by which Ahab furnishes the whale's meaning) depends the definition of choice, the conditions of liberty, and the entire problem of the relation of will to appetite and inclination.

But where does the whale figure in all this? Even if it ensures a certain discomfiture, consider the *Leviathan* as a guide: in strictly mathematical terms man enters into a commonwealth, willingly giving up some personal freedoms for the guarantee of protection under the name of a sovereign power. Hobbes's formula amounts to the logical conclusion that the partial loss of self through allegiance to a king is preferable to the total loss of self to the bloody enemy. But the real compromise of the commonwealth is a philosophical one, and Hobbes was perhaps the first to put it in writing. Gone will be the pure brutality of survival, of man against man, from the earth's surface. But in exchange one must admit that such divisive forces exist. Everywhere man will be free, and everywhere he will be in chains—only those chains will be the invisible drives that propel and thwart his desires. It is a picture of civil war going underground, or into the human body, where its implosion no longer draws blood but results instead in the implicit understanding of the fragmented nature of man—evident in work from Shakespeare to Picasso, from psychoanalysis to the splitting of the atom to the postmodern novel.

Complicating the thrill of independence, then, is the hard truth of contract. A social state is one in which members must contract to agree in terms on which they don't agree. It is a built state as opposed to a found state. Artificial, since it is made, but artificial in the way that nature is artificial; engineered, in other words—the ever-changing result of serendipitous and provocative pressures on its design. As a consequence of this newfound dependence on terms, the most marked effect of the commonwealth is to make language the site of contention. In a social state words take on a life of their own, which is one reason why founders or makers of nations are necessarily writers. They understand that being political means putting their lives on the line.

Hobbes prefaces the modern attention to semantics, which means he abandons any sense that language stands in for things or represents things. The kingdom of the Leviathan does not offer any dusty imprints, from which it is possible to trace the path between words and real objects. Ours is a world which, since its beginning (begun, as it were, at its first word), is wet—all slick surfaces and slippery slopes. This tenuous surface demands the most versatile conveyance. Where labels fail us, Hobbes seems to suggest, the floating alphabet does not. As he says, "The invention of *Printing*, though ingenious, compared with the invention of *Letters*, is no great matter."

Distilled, tidy, and a natural preservative, language is indispensable to man's precarious journey. Words are the craftiest means of conveyance we have, and human survival depends on them. If words are to be of any use, though, they must somehow be reliable—not by way of an anchor (latching on to something solid and dependable) but in the way of a compass and sextant. Words are not timeless, unchronicled occasions; they take place in the context of particular acts of attention. In the case of sailors a good example of this kind of accountability is Greenwich Mean Time. Though its location in England privileges a particular perspective, there is no illusion that the designated time has any relation to God. It is simply a point, pulled from an infinite number of points, for the purpose of establishing a means by which to locate other points—ships—in relation to each other. To locate perspective one needs a basis for consideration, a foundation on which to establish position. In the grand map of the world, what allows a sea captain to say "I am here" is a selected collection of numbers: latitude, longitude,

Greenwich Mean Time. Nobody would dispute the *reality* of a ship, but the ability to articulate its whereabouts is made available by a code, agreed upon by man, signed into contract by sailors, who make possible the truth of their positions through the lie of their coordinates.

There are certain rules, a kind of livable code, that keeps humans afloat in this suddenly wide and watery world. The name for this contingency, called by Hobbes *Leviathan*, is the name by which we hold ourselves together—a term denoting both the state of our society and the state of our persons. It is an act that needs to be contrived, though to call it counterfeit sounds strange. It is a freedom that exists under the restraints of its body. Philosophically Leviathan is a *condition*. It is the structuring movement of countless, invisible forces. And like pregnancy or ocean travel it is apt to cause nausea, the feeling of being at once stationary and mobile. An author schooled by the Leviathan knows there is a science, what one might call a social science, to the strange domain that is at once cohesive and flexible, a state that is not a thing so much as a dimension.

To the contemplation of this dimension, though, one must add ethical considerations. Some feminists, for instance, have found troubling implications in the sexless, featureless quality of the body politic. In the morphological correspondence between the artificial commonwealth and the human body, Elizabeth Grosz has asked, "What takes on the metaphoric function of the genitals? And what kind of genitals are they?" In addition to the implicitly masculine, unrecognized encoding of the body politic, the lack of any real fleshy substance gives the whole enterprise a kind of slippery quality; to what, in such a state, does one hold on to? To whom does one turn for justice?

In a watery world survival depends on certain guidelines, and these bearings are to be taken on the open independence of the sea. But there must be a real body implicated in the process, from whom we can extract promises, gain succor; in whom we can take comfort; on whose solid shape we can depend, lay claim. In time of need, the shore is apt to splinter any fragile transport—in a gale, the land is a ship's direst jeopardy—but whale flesh is surer anchorage for the sailor in search of something to fasten on to. A whale is a seaman's version of coming to rest, a fisherman's paradise, Milton's most solid something in the inconstant oceans of the planet: "Leviathan, / Hugest of living creatures, in the deep / Stretch'd like a promontory sleeps or swims, / And seems a moving land; and at his gills / Draws in, and at his breath spouts out a sea."

A whale is no easy consolation, however; to come upon him is to confront the sublime. Alongside the imposing creature, a whaler may be reminded of his own insufficiencies and limitations—but he is buoyed by the sense that his rational faculty, at least, swells to encompass the beast. The astonishment and delirium provoked by such an encounter is commonplace to whalers, who are more privy than most to the grotesque, erotic, uproarious ability of man's contemplative capacity. But even the bravest of whalemen cannot help but be nonplussed. As Ahab cries: "O soul of man! how far beyond all utterance are your linked analogies! not the smallest atom stirs or lives in matter, but has its cunning duplicate in mind."

If such a cry is normally beyond the ability of human utterance, how to make it palatable, tame it to the stuff of smart, polite conversation? As one of three epigraphs that make up *Moby Dick*'s "Etymology," Melville has chosen the following from Hackluyt:

> While you take in hand to school others, and to teach them by what name a whale-fish is to be called in our tongue, leaving out, through ignorance, the letter H, which almost alone maketh up the signification of the word, you deliver that which is not true.

In Melville's own unschooled American mouth, "whale" *would* have sounded like "wail." The author, educated on a whale ship (or at least not, like Hackluyt, at Oxford's Christchurch College), certainly had it in mind to "school others" about the whale business. There seems a kind of constitutional motivation behind Melville's choosing, but not honoring, Hackluyt's warning. How can man endure the tremendous creative responsibility of living in a world seemingly written into being with words of his own choosing? Advice from the upper class would include careful pronunciation—the inclusion of the scholar's *H*. With the proper precautions it is possible to reduce man's *wail* (that Copernican echo, the noise a human makes on discovery that his hope of finding refuge in the world is in vain—he is himself his world) into a *whale*. What is overwhelming in its boundarylessness can be shrunk to a hefty, blubber-coated, but manageable size.

In this story the whale is not man's foe but his foil, a certain solid something he can position himself against. Here layers of fat and muscle preserve, even as they threaten, human ability to cross the sea. In a great blue basin with no paths or guidelines across it, the body of the whale provides the tension and friction that is necessary to move. As if the amount of water it displaces is just enough to invoke the memory of land. Two-thirds of the world's mass is ocean, Melville reminds his readers, and ships are but splinters on its waves. On the open sea, swimming sailors hug the body of their crafts, knowing that for a figure alone in the water it does not take long for madness to set in. More seaworthy than a boat, the reassuring girth of the whale battles human agoraphobia. To further justify the relationship, whalers project malevolence onto their prey. If the fish has a temper, even better reason for whalers' furious pursuit, holding onto the whales for dear life *as if* they were encompassing them in the arms of death.

If real progress is at stake (like the kind that gets one from here to there, without drowning on the way), then there needs to be a sea-bound contract, something one can count on: two hundred barrels of oil; four missing men; one lost leg; the three hundredth lay. Such is the sober balance of sublime possibility. Not only helpful but necessary are the mundane drudgeries that distract us from the vision that fleetingly presents itself. It's a long road from here to there, and we must keep on it.

Ahab is acquainted with the first leg of the journey. He knows that even though he has won from his men a promise to kill Moby Dick, the beauty of such a plan will conflict with human allegiance to the daily grind: "In times of strong emotion mankind disdain all base considerations; but such times are evanescent. The permanent constitutional condition of the manufactured man, thought Ahab, is sordidness." If Ahab wants to keep his men on what he considers the true quest of the white whale, he will have to provide food for their daily appetites through the regular business of lowering for all sperm whales. He does not make the mistake of underestimating the whalers' desire for profit. On consideration, he supposes that these mild impediments to his design will help ensure the continued loyalty of his men: "Had they been strictly held to their one final and romantic object—that final and romantic object, too many would have turned from in disgust."

While *Moby Dick*'s governing device is the capture of the white whale, its author has his own "final and romantic object," one too many would turn from in disgust without the distractions of writerly equivalencies of cash—action and adventure, blood and vanity and betrayal. The chapter of Ahab's scheming, called "Surmises," is followed by the first lowering, the supposed action of the novel. The disturbing suggestion is that this novel's readers have contracted for a voyage whose real object is unclear. In "The Pequod Meets the Albatross," which turns out to be not a bird but a ship, a crew of strangely quiet sailors refuse to answer the *Pequod*'s questions. It is at this crucial juncture that the readers of *Moby Dick* should begin to feel the weight of a shared burden, even if it is a feather weight. As the *Pequod* and the *Albatross* glide by each other, fish and philosophy realign themselves:

> At that moment the two wakes were fairly crossed, and instantly, then, in accordance with their singular ways, shoals of small harmless fish, that for some days before had been placidly swimming by our side, darted away with what seemed shuddering fins, and ranged themselves fore and aft with the stranger's flanks. Though in the course of his continual voyagings Ahab must often before have noticed a similar sight, yet, to any monomaniac man, the veriest trifles capriciously carry meanings.
> "Swim away from me, do ye?" murmured Ahab, gazing over into the water. There seemed but little in the words, but the tone conveyed more of deep helpless sadness than the insane old man had ever before evinced. But turning to the steersman . . . he cried out in his old lion voice,—"Up helm! Keep her off round the world!"
> Round the world! There is much in that sound to inspire proud feelings: but whereto does all that circumnavigation conduct? Only through numberless perils to

the very point whence we started, where those that we left behind secure, were all the time before us.

Circling the world and slaughtering whales is only so much sea biscuit in between leaving home and finding oneself home again, with the old original self-reckoning still due. Which may mean that whale killing is only the distraction of this book, its sexy sideline, and not its romantic object.

Moby Dick, in all his particular, albino glory, is plucked from some abstract and serviceable whale populace and brought to life in this specific story—so that he is ordinary and in circulation, not representative and exempted from it. The men on board the *Pequod* are real-life whalers, not mythical Sailors, and they know what it's like to scrub decks and boil blubber, to sweat and stink and miss their wives. In the world of *Moby Dick,* the whale is just a whale. But boiling down that mass into five small letters, readers should remember that Leviathan is a condition, or state, to which we are party. The reader of *Moby Dick,* at the end of the line, is bound to find out the truth. Reading the whale means reading our destiny. Would a whale by any other name smell as sweet? Reading is not the process of seeing something in the world, retaining its image, and matching the appropriate label. We don't need to witness something to talk about it (as Ishmael points out, the world talks about whales when few people have lived to see them and tell about it). In *Moby Dick* the whale is not a symbol; it is man who is symbolic. The novel's author seems to be suggesting that since man is a symbolic species, the work to be done is not whale killing but whale reading. Using the designation w h a l e is what we do, whether we have firsthand knowledge of the beast or not.

Whale reading, like its more material cousin whale hunting, is no light undertaking. Reading the whale is "a ponderous task; no ordinary letter-sorter in the Post Office is equal to it. To grope down into the bottom of the sea after them; to have one's hands among the unspeakable foundations, ribs, and very pelvis of the world; this is a fearful thing." It is an act of creation. This work sounds conspiratorial, unsanctified. Groping among parts, ribs and pelvises, means having a hand in the assembly of "this . . . fearful thing." The fright that comes after such crafting is not the result of vain overreaching but a dawning understanding of the human condition. Says this thing's author: "The awful tauntings in Job might well appall me. 'Will he' (the leviathan) 'make a covenant with thee?' Behold the hope of him is vain!" The most awful taunt to Job is, finally, that God will not answer him. Or God's answer is that there is no answer. God need not explain himself or engage in manly discussion. Job's patience comes from his understanding that even though, unprovoked, God punished him, still God cannot be looked to for an explanation for his behavior: "For he is not a man, as I am, / that I should answer him, / and we should come together in judgment." The covenant of language, which is a burden even as it grants unprecedented privilege, is man's alone. Definitions and explanations are, sadly, earthly responsibilities. Melville, bound and tied by his human sentence, can joke that even the whale descriptions that are included in his cetology folio have no godly connection to the beast. Like those terms that he dismisses from his lexicon (elephant whale, scragg whale), the suspicion is that he can "hardly help suspecting them for mere sounds, full of Leviathanism, but signifying nothing."

Up again, old heart. This creation business is brave and fool-hardy, guaranteed of failure and some strange success. Melville makes a career (almost) out of showing how he can use the word *whale.* His is a practice that can be undertaken only by some-one who forges as he investigates, who pushes and pursues his subject, who comes to it from a hundred different angles and, seeing it in bits and pieces, assembles the thing under the conditions created in the course of writing, which is the only means by which to give it life. Although his whale cannot be understood by means of a dictionary, Melville's readers, forced to see the same word hundreds of times in continually chang-ing contexts, will learn the meaning of the word in relation to the world.

But unlike the definitions of words one learns at school, a seaman's approach to language is vulnerable to the charge of error, as it has to pay for its affection for the open seas and in-tellectual complexity with the loss of its credentials. No security can be found in an ocean that refuses to memorialize where man has been. All that work over this one word, *whale,* is ac-complished by any number of words, four hundred pages of words, that seem to require no explanation. Which means that all Meville's efforts toward making *whale* a public word produce only very small inroads against the argument that words are finally private, or that readers may only pretend to share, but not really share, the meanings of words. And if words are private, constitutions are meaningless. Heroic effort on Melville's part might mean that *whale* is one word whose meaning may be known, but it is only one word. If all words are to be proved public (so that one may live or die by them, be guided or lost by them, remain connected to the world, or battle skepticism, because of them), some other strategy must be discovered, some more killer instinct enlisted, which outlasts all intention exactly because it does not become obsessed with foundations and instead proceeds directly and instinctively toward its certain goal.

{ 2 }

A Common Account of Shipping

I am as low and befuddled as any man, as fouled
and out of touch and self-deluded; this is what gives me
a place from which to speak.

—*Charles Bernstein,* My Way

TO SHIP IS NOT AN INDEPENDENT AND PRIVATE EVENT
but, like consciousness, a catalog of material engagement with
the world. It is not independent because any sea-bound vessel
floats on a supportive sea (even though the bedrock of this support is conditional, a vague hope at the bottom of an impossible
depth). It is not private because like all phenomenal experience it is hampered by connection to the world, to wind and
wave. Under sail a ship can never take the shape of an objective
narrative but must remain an interpretation of its own influence and association.

As Pacific anthropologist Greg Dening says, space and the
language used to describe it are what make up a ship. A ship is
a particular, peculiar contrivance: it entails confined quarters
and suffocating proximity; theatrical, ambiguous authority (a
captain's word was law, and his laws were subject to his moods);
the continuous feeling of rising above impossible odds. Like a
poem, a ship gestures in the direction of certain genre conven-
tions and it cannot or should not divorce its meaning from its
practice. Time spent on ships provisions the need for new calcula-
tions concerning the navigation of worldly territory—navigation
that promises to be less progressive than poetic. In this new

world there is order, but it is an order that cannot be *drawn*—at least it can't depend for its cartography on a geographic model. More appealing than the solid account of enumerated distances known as geography, to those who ship, is the science of nearness and rifts, a seaman's science. Reformulating space along sailors' lines means losing patience with simple definitions of *next to, following, and then, and so.* Replacing old contiguities are new affinities.

As Foucault says in *The Order of Things,* this new science nets "fragments of a large number of possible orders." Here they "glitter separately . . . without law or geometry." It is with glitter that this next chapter deals, for which it must venture at least partway into the world of alchemy. Is the maxim "All is not gold that glitters" a scientific or philosophical warning? Or is it less a warning than a clue? If Foucault's fragmented, glittering order is one without geometry, or is independent of linear, measured sequence, does that mean it is without law? To maintain order without law is to envision some other ingenious system, some organizing force both independent and particular, both public and personal. To go looking for a categorical imperative of this kind sounds suspiciously like a search for fool's gold. But perhaps such an expedition would not be so different from thinking one could find a whale in all the great wetness of the sea.

The practice of shipping as a whale hunter must have seemed an absurd and preposterous act: to set forth, an odd crew of boys and men, underwashed, poorly schooled, in a complicated arrangement of hemp, cotton, and planks, upon the open ocean. To watch the surface of these watery wastes for signs that may or may not signal the presence of a free-swimming creature hidden beneath the waves. To correctly predict where the colossal mammal will surface, to row a small boat, back-first, toward it, and, if it can be gained on, to try to puncture it with a metal shaft slightly longer than a man's leg, tied to a line, tied to the man. To kill it in this manner, to strap it to the side of a ship not much bigger in length, to peel from it fishy strips of fat and boil this product until it becomes edible, burnable, bathable. It seems hugely arrogant to expect even to find the creatures, yet such arrogance lit up a world.

The oily "black gold" of the whaling industry certainly proved that booty lurked in strange places, and it took a kind of foolhardiness to get there. To make philosophy of the practice might mean saying that a genuine search for fool's gold is one way of reformulating questions of value. Is it foolish to confuse something that looks like gold *for* gold—or is it a fool who looks for gold where it isn't expected to be found? Does gold welcome fools gladly? Gold is somehow that unadulterated thing that can only be found but not made—it is impervious to the laws of matter and need. If gold is the measure of value that exists above or outside of the law of circumstance, how foolish would it be to try one's hand at gold making and so complicate such a model? (So that its categorical quality is tempered by the importunity of an imperative, by urgency and necessity?) Does "All that glitters is not gold" simply mean I can dance around the living room in my underwear, but it doesn't make me Madonna—or more profoundly, could it genuinely suggest there is that besides gold which glitters, that there is value outside the established bar, a more fluid, invested kind of worth?

In *Moby Dick*, those who look for gold are made foolish, while those who look for fool's gold find success. In the chapter called "The Gilder," gold is the hue reminiscent of solidity, the color of a sunny ocean so calm a man floating on its surface "feels a certain filial, confident, land-like feeling towards the sea . . . he regards it as so much flowery earth." This rolling prairie provokes mystic projection, and a lulled sailor can "almost swear that play-wearied children lie sleeping in these solitudes, in some glad May-time, when the flowers of the woods are plucked." But confusing the sea for land is dangerous practice. The sea, Ahab knows, is deceptive. He can't look upon a gilded sea without recalling its dark underside:

> If these secret golden keys did seem to open in him his own secret golden treasuries, yet did his breath upon them prove but tarnishing.
> Oh grassy glades! . . . Would to God these blessed calms would last. But the mingled, mingling threads of life are woven by warp and woof: calm crossed by storms, a storm for every calm.

Ahab's panting world-weariness reveals gold leaf to be so much shine on a shifting, unmanageable surface. Unwilling to follow his captain's lead, Starbuck, skilled enough to see the seduction, is nevertheless ready to trade knowledge for comfort:

> And that same day, too, gazing far down from his boat's side into that same golden sea, Starbuck lowly murmured:—
> "Loveliness unfathomable, as ever lover saw in his young bride's eye!—Tell me not of thy teeth-tiered sharks, and thy kidnapping cannibal ways. Let faith oust fact; let fancy oust memory; I look deep down and do believe."

But it is the peculiar mate Stubb who perverts Starbuck's rooted dream and Ahab's watery nightmare, who interrupts the sailors' reverie with his own, fishy-glittery third possibility:

> And Stubb, fish-like, with sparkling scales, leaped up in that same golden light:—
> "I am Stubb, and Stubb has his history; but here Stubb takes oaths that he has always been jolly!"

This strange ejaculation appears to point to some undetected evolutionary line, some vein of fool's gold for which, in reading *Moby Dick,* it seems worthwhile to search. The trade will be to abandon continental geography, the measured step from here to there, as it is suitable for plains, not seas. Like real gold, that kind of weighty standard can be counted on, but it is on loan from the frozen space of the vault. More true to a whaling life will be a study of nearness and rifts, a process closer to that which turns words into literature, or acquaintances into friends.

Melville did know a real-life gold hunter, a man whose influence has been hard to trace. He was a whaler, a failure, and a fool, and if anyone can be credited with Melville's introduction to the glories of alchemy, he can't. Melville meets him when he clambers aboard the weedy whaling rig *Julia* after fleeing the Marquesas. They part in Eimeo, Tahiti—Melville to go on to Honolulu and work in a bowling alley, his friend (pockets full of Melville's money) to spend some time hunting nuggets in San Francisco and Australia. This man, whom Melville brings to the page in *Omoo,* provides a kind of model for surveying in

Moby Dick. Dr. Long Ghost, the Ghost, fleshy spectacle John B. Troy, teaches Melville how to find treasure in unexpected places. The benefit of following his practice is that the doctor's type of poetic alchemy—or finding value in the valueless—can show how such art is a dignified science.

Showing that the search for fool's gold is a viable scientific practice is important because reading *Moby Dick* well, or let's say attentively, is to respond to a new kind of relation between science and art. *Moby Dick* is literature caught in the act of its own consideration, literature become wary, alert. This kind of writing is precarious because the materials of its construction are also the means of its rescue. In an ordinary sense, this simply means it has become philosophy. As such it is both art and science. The accomplishment of *art* is to make the familiar unfamiliar; by provoking the sleepy eye to retrace its path it startles a reader or witness into participation. To be artistic is to be awake. The accomplishment of *science* is to bring the world together in such a way that it can be acted on, or acted in. Science tries to find ways to proceed methodically, from one point to the next—but it also necessarily concerns itself with the forces that guide attraction and repulsion, how things come together or split apart. To be scientific means to notice states of arousal, the call one substance has on another, the response of a body to a particular circumstance. Literature that becomes philosophy is writing that is both awake and aroused. Interested in making the familiar strange and vice versa, it also does not neglect impulses that betray relations—signs of the entangled, implicated nature of matter.

In *The Order of Things* Foucault sets up the difference between science and literature by suggesting that the sciences "always carry within themselves the project, however remote it may be, of an exhaustive ordering of the world; they are always directed, too, towards the discovery of simple elements and their progressive combination." Certainly the humanities have been exhausted by the declaration that precision and veracity can only be maintained through careful, cumulative agglomeration, where small fact steps upon small fact until we find ourselves on the moon. Such a path long ago provoked poets to announce the moon was made of cheese. The contention of those preoccupied with language is that unearthing the rhetorical dimension of words (that words are not labels for things but go boldly where no man has gone before) discovers the freedom of the sign to alight on some absent point. A move more profound and far-reaching than any careful tracking can hope to follow.

The "science" to which the humanities casually refer, however, seems to be the science whose preoccupation with *function* gave way to considerations of *structure*—or what is known as basic chemistry, the problems of molecular architecture. As critics of this branch of science were quick to point out, the approach is above all quantitative, a process of measuring substances and restricting study to that which can be measured. But this modest and methodical understanding of properties need not be the model against which language philosophers prepare their arguments. Worming its way through the history of science has been the question posed by Aristotle and the Stoics: What holds bodies together? What attracts and impels, what inclines? This interest in attraction is not the challenge poets have put to science but one science has put to itself. It is here at this juncture of science and poetry (not where they meet, as in complement, but where they are the same) that philosophy can avoid being reduced to commentary and can begin to act creatively.

Dr. Long Ghost models creative science (one could call this literature, or alchemy, depending on the mood) because his interests are conditional and associative. He borrows this classical approach from natural philosophy, which aimed to identify what fundamental components made up material objects as well as explain how the world came to be organized—why this and not that, how sea from land from sky. Those who sailed with Long Ghost may have found him wanting as a physician (he stole drugs from the supply chest, ignored the sick captain and "treated" himself), but his physics are superb. His practice shows evidence of knowing that the accuracy of science's ability to explain the *construction* of matter grows in proportion to its ability to explain the *inclination* of matter. In other words, Long Ghost intuits the lessons of quantum mechanics. Innovation in this area came about not through dazzling feats of objectivity but by way of investment and implication.

Instead of exhibiting a procrustean disregard for special circumstances and relationships, those whose interest in organized bodies proved fruitful began by paying better attention to the vernacular landscape. The landscape, in this case, is more like the spread of an ocean. Whalers and physicists share the same methodology; each is interested in undercurrents, the pull and tug on a body that is not obvious to the naked eye. In fact, following the transformation of atomic to subatomic theory (the first suggestions of which were thought by many to resemble a search for fool's gold) sounds a lot like a whale hunt. Influenced by the teachings of Pythagoras, early formulations of atomism imagined "uncuttable" bits made of the same basic material, atoms, floating in a void where they could affect one another only by interlocking or colliding. But the internal logic of purely atomistic theory prohibits it from explaining organized bodies or directed activity. Early atomists saw living things as unusually large collections of atoms that glommed together, by chance, stayed together for a lifetime, and then— again by chance—fell apart. But according to this model, how is anything found, made, made again? Theoretically atomism relies either on chance or on some external order to make it cohesive, which turns an organized body into either a mighty accident or a miracle.

Because living things showed clear evidence of design, some theories of matter seemed to solve the problem by taking an ungainly side-step shuffle into the fields of the miraculous. Plato, a geometrician, consigned the unchartable influences of organization to the divine force. Organization was decreed at creation, when maps of the future, or blueprints, were put into circulation. Even Newton, whose theories are more familiar to a modern understanding, follows this pattern of conceiving atoms as providing the building materials from which the Divine Architect constructed the perfectly planned world. But the difference between Newton's atomism (particularly in his theory of gravity) and earlier versions lies in his additional attention to a continuous, dynamic agency responsible for upholding the cohesion of the body. A system of attractions and repulsions. This agency is not provided externally or encountered accidentally but is at work internally, is implicated in the nature of bodies.

The tracings of this other influence are interesting to a whaler or sailor for whom strictly geometrical maps offer dubious direction. All along, while some scientists puzzled out shapes, others were more interested in forces. Working in his favorite field of marine biology, Aristotle ran into problems when he tried to define animals on the basis of abstract behavior and not on organs and fluids. "It is evidently not *shapes* that mark the different elementary substances off from one another," he wrote, but rather the functions and capacities that lie in their bodies. The Stoics agreed that for organized systems there must be more organic explanations than accident or angels, but they found these "integral properties" to derive not from the solids and liquids of a body but from something they called the *pneuma*. There must be something in man, they were sure, that is more than the sum of his various parts. As Toulmin and Goodfield quip in *The Architecture of Matter,* "Whereas, for instance, a man's weight is the sum of his various organs, his glumness is not the sum of their respective glumnesses." Something like attraction, or tension, can't be weighed or measured and is not in itself an additional ingredient—it is a *state* or *condition.* An untuned piano produces a cacophonous, not melodious, sound, yet none of its materials have changed. A woman who has just received a threatening phone call will respond differently to a knock at the door.

Science was left with these two polarized positions. Early atomism suggested that accidental impact and contact were what created material objects, that geometry alone could teach us the shape of the world. These mechanical explanations were promising and satisfying but necessitated some step outside themselves in order to hold together, a step toward God or a supplicating shrug in the direction of coincidence. The continuum theories of the Stoics focused attention on the fact that bodies *do* hold together, that some other activating force impels and provokes material objects. But they were plagued by an impractical sense of all matter making its eventual headway toward some graceful goal and thus glossed over real accident and innovation, the useful truths of mechanical engineering.

Alchemy negotiated the solution—and in the process turned science into an art. Here craftsmen married their articulate working knowledge of matter to the fluid clarity of Greek philosophy, whose truths had been made watery by a disregard for demonstrable facts. Aristotle's principle of development, that all things mature and change into a certain ripeness, lent itself as a lens through which materials of the earth could be seen in their "living" form. So instead of thinking matter to be static or inert, men thought of even gold and silver in a physiological way. The earth was seen as a womb in which materials were conceived and gestated. Until the eighteenth century, it was even believed that mined veins would undertake their own underground regeneration.

Such talk, while sounding funny to modern ears, was in fact layered with scrupulous and wide-ranging knowledge of chemistry. The metallurgical techniques of later centuries come principally from alchemical sources. But because their understanding of chemical change was bound up with creation, it is easy to see how alchemists attracted enemies like flies to baklava. Christian theologians regarded the practice as impious; later scientists found it tainted by the gross myths of religion. But what should be interesting is that alchemy produced a new kind of fruit (or fruitcake), a third option that did not suffer from the divorce between practice and theory, or the fact that the world was made up of bits and that it still somehow came together in particular ways.

Because alchemy's most famous quackery is the attempt to make gold from less precious metals, it seems fair to take this attempt on its own terms. Gold's embryological status sounds like a joke. But because alchemists conceived of nature as performing certain operations on minerals that they could try to reproduce, they inserted into chemistry an attention to conditions, to ambiance. *If* the compound was free of putridness, the practitioner's soul pure, the temperature conducive, the room sealed, then the desired goings-on might occur. Not only did such solicitous attention help provide the peculiarly careful stagings of science, but they must also have reinserted that old circumstantial, biological, Aristotelian, mythic sense of things inseparable from their world, things coming into their own, things undergoing some sort of evolutionary process.

It is interesting to think about the fruitfulness of the alchemists' search. If attempting to make gold is a failure, it is surely the type of failure that Melville finds his constant consort and companion. Fool's gold (that thought to be precious when it is not, he who thinks to find sureness where he cannot) is somehow implicated in the process of inserting value into a well-panned world. There is something heroic about the insistence that all is not lost, or found, but that it can be made. There is something terribly sophisticated and terribly practical about fool's gold. It is a fruitful failure. It's a joke whose punch line is to set the world's dreadful failings in some kind of sunny, beneficial light. All does not depend on what you find but is in some way responsive to what you make. You can either make chicken shit, or chicken salad.

This strange foolishness is a counter to the death knell some critics have supposed *Moby Dick* to be ringing. Sophisticated in its watery analogies, unblinking in its dissection of sham landscapes, *Moby Dick* still retains a philosophy close to classical alchemy. Its interests are creative, its poetics engaged in the construction of something valuable. In *Moby Dick* Melville cleaves to poetic models, which put more faith in making than finding, or that imagine making as a kind of finding. This ingenuity depends on a quasi certainty about how to proceed, or at least how to dispatch crippling despondency. But if what makes *Moby Dick* coherent is confidence, not despair, then from what direction does this influence come? One contestant is the man to whom much of Melville's immunity to despair is owed—Doctor Long Ghost.

Immunity, of course, is not imperviousness but comes from exposure. To be immune to despair is to carry a part of it with you, to take it seriously as a threat and condition. And then, once proofed in this way, carrying your defense in your belly, *to run amuck.* No one carries immunity to sickness like doctors, because they live in close proximity to all its rank foulness. Doctor Long Ghost, the Ghost, the Long Doctor, "treats" his "patient" Melville, who has no apparent ailment but is nevertheless suffering. Treating Melville is possible because of the doctor's own exposure—but what is this unnamed, unmanning angst that needs ministering to?

The beginning of Melville's literary career coincides with the end of his short stay in the Pacific. As a young sailor, he abandons a wretched life on a stinking whale ship in favor of the Marquesan island of Nuku Hiva—where, although he is treated in princely fashion, he leaves in a fit of violence in order to return to a wretched life on a stinking whale ship. In character (Tommo, of *Typee*) and in desperation, Melville climbs from the gentle coconut-scented arms of Fayaway and the manly embrace of Kory-Kory onto the vile, rat-infested hull of yet another whalers' rig, the *Lucy-Ann* or in real-time the *Julia*—and why, exactly? He smashes a man in the face with a boat hook in order to leave the islands, indicating that his flight and fright are serious. But what has he left that's so sickening? Perhaps what horrified him was the possibilty of losing himself. (In *Typee* he calls his dread the fear of cannibalism, but what is cannibalism's threat if not the threat of losing oneself?) What Melville suffered from—having been forced to concede the false choice of Typee or Happar, cannibal or Christian; after enduring a sailor's sunburn and watching the skin peel off only to find the same skin and watch it snake off again as if he were some shedding onion; after watching the sea *looking for whales*—was the threat of a strained expectation into nothing. A purposelessness and feeling of being out of place when one has done nothing different and yet everything is different.

For the illness Melville discovers in the valley of the Typees— that which left him spinning out of control, abandoning paradise with the force of a man run out of options—Doctor Long Ghost knows the prescription. What the young sailor encounters that's so restorative, on board the *Julia,* is the strange, strained laugh of the doctor. What greets his unexplained flight from paradise, his haunted eye, his desperation to ship out, is a humorous reception. How could treating desperation as a joke be any kind of cure? "In everything that is to excite a lively convulsive laugh," says Kant, in the *Critique of Judgement,* "there must be something absurd (in which the understanding, therefore, can find no satisfaction). *Laughter is an affection arising from the sudden transformation of a strained expectation into nothing.*" One way to name what the doctor offered Melville is immunity—a shared suck at the teat of ill-parenting disillusion, but not enough to poison. Just enough to recognize the enemy as sometime friend, to see the joke of having not known where to go next, having not seen the punch line before it tripped you up, as itself a bit of a saving grace. Freshly arrived on deck, wobbly and wild-eyed from his first extended voyage across the beach, Melville finds the one thing that can save him—a man who has seen it all and has been able to *go on* in a certain way. And as a result, the fear lurking behind those famously small brown eyes, the despondency of a man adrift, eases into something more relaxed, a more manageable partnership with incredulity.

Traces of Long Ghost are available; apart from his detailed stint on board the *Julia* and time spent with Melville in Tahiti, signs reveal him to be looking for riches in San Francisco, and also in the goldfields of Australia. Rumor has it that Melville hears from him again by letter, just as the author is struggling through the writing of *Moby Dick,* when Long Ghost takes it upon himself to remind his old friend that what is needed is not a successful travel narrative but a subversive book. The best place to find the Long Doctor, however, is in the pages of Ian Wedde's novel exploration of the underbelly of official history in the Pacific, *Symmes Hole.*

New Zealand–born Wedde—poet, dramatist, and now concept curator for the Museum of New Zealand—pictures Long Ghost through a South Seas lens. Wedde's waggish doctor "takes drugs from his own medicine supply . . . pulls off outrageous practical jokes . . . never does a stroke of work . . . drinks the captain's brandy on the pretext of being there to 'Doctor' him." But what he provides is a strange calm in the craziness of the Pacific, "where annexations occur like grotesque practical jokes; where sadists and criminals have God on their side; where Civilization loads grape and chain to howl forth from the muzzles of sixty-eight pounders to scythe down bamboo walls behind which children are hiding in the belief that being out of sight is some guarantee of safety . . . *ha ha.*" In the face of this "insane charade," what the Long Ghost offers, says Wedde, is some perspective: "What Long Ghost has, is an Overview. Oh, he's no moral hero—in fact, he turns out to be immoral, exploitative, selfish, etc etc. But somehow he manages to not give offense, except when he means to, which is rarely. And he has the knack of showing people where they are."

Into the glittery world Long Ghost does not hurl himself with a rock tied to his waist, like Ahab, nor betray his senses in some corporate plea for order, like Starbuck. Instead he spreads madness, enjoys articulation and his cultured, well-bred witticisms, doesn't underestimate the bodily pleasures—booze, a plug of tobacco, a backroom fondle—and in this ordinary way undermines the fatalistic dread that can accompany any savvy appraisal. Predecessor to Stubb, Long Ghost is no grand philosopher, no notable model, but he does show the comical toughness of one who has had to deal with the demands of survival with nothing at hand but his own handiness. To Melville such a man imparts a sanity made from the scrap stuff of sea life: a smoke, the view from the rigging, shore leave, the impression of tides, the comforting stink of men's bodies in a closed room. His direction is less like advice than a wink—as if you already comprehend whatever it is he could say. The Long Ghost of *Symmes Hole* knows that in the face of the charade parade, a man who takes sides is bound to come unbalanced. What you have to be is "an anarchist to whom this authority is meaningless":

> You have to see health as more than fitness. You have to be unafraid and therefore without respect . . . without pride and therefore without anger . . . unprejudiced, and therefore unpredictable, or plain mad . . . without interests or power and therefore unimpressed by talk of justice . . . incorrupt and therefore a *failure.*
> Something has begun to open up in Herman's mind.
> . . . your mind must be like the lagoon of an atoll: through the break in the reef which protects its tranquility, the tides pass in and out—the flood of the wide ocean, the ebb of the enclosure. . . . the flood, and the ebb: you'll be without unilateral convictions, you won't need confidence.

A sensitive sailor who cannot adjust to the impartial rockings of the ocean is candidate for nausea. More gravely, one who cannot loosen the grip on his convictions (and so becomes tangled in the crosshatch of competing stories) is bound for shipwreck.

When Melville takes his acquaintance with Long Ghost earnestly, or when he makes an investment in him by giving the Ghost's influence a kind of literary life, he recognizes a coping mechanism more secure than any vessel. Long Ghost may be a hack, but his disrespect for authority never congeals into the kind of righteousness that can weigh down a buoyant enterprise. He is, as Wedde reveals him, a "teacher" for whom instruction is at best boring and unimaginative, at worst deadly. Experienced enough to recognize the dreadful seriousness of the situation, the Ghost knows that to throw serious at serious is like pitching oil on flame. The Melville who fled the Marquesas was all equipped to reveal, with the solemnity of the newly exposed, his battle scars. (Missionaried hypocrisies. Civilized Western savageries.) But as the successful ringleader of rebellion on the *Julia,* Dr. Long Ghost knows there is nothing like straightforward testimony to neuter a mutiny before it really gets going. That defiance is a little more complicated, a little more ridiculous—even absurd—is Long Ghost's lesson:

> Doctor Long Ghost's no Messiah . . . at the same time, he never pretends to be anything but a *tourist* in paradise. He is incorrupt like a sore cleaned by maggots. And although he wouldn't waste what contempt he's capable of on notions of evangelism or the passing on of wisdom, he becomes Herman's Teacher. He's not as subtle as the Zen Master who said to his "brilliant" student, "Before your cup can be full, first it must be empty!"—The Ghost swipes Herman's share, probably when he's not looking, and drinks it at a gulp. . . . so what?—Herman's cup is empty . . . he spends some weeks in Tahiti with fewer fears, and more suspension of judgments, and having more fun, than at any other time in his life.
>
> No doubt about it, John B. Troy is the loony, disrespectful squire who prepares the Dark Knight for his Sombre Quest . . . he's the crazy Zen Master who beats the shit out of this "brilliant" young dark-eyed student . . . he's the Mad Shrink who screams with laughter at the woeful revelations of his brooding patient . . . he's the Casting Director who yells at the "promising" young serious actor, "Hey you! *Make a noise like a tomato!* "

To understand how this spirit influences science (why one should look to a ghost doctor for help) is to get an inkling of how at a certain point science and literature shared the same discoveries. In the nineteenth century, models of the atom (and thus the structure of how the world held together) still retained a mechanical quality. It was thought that the workings of material bodies could be explained by a picture, and that reality resembled very closely what the picture led one to suspect. To break the mold took fools and absurdists, who introduced a series of hypotheses that changed investigative direction. More cosmological than logical, innovations like J. J. Thompson's discovery of the electron cracked and fissured an early atomic model—plaguing mechanical conclusions by encouraging the return of questions surrounding the nature of cohesion. No longer unchangeable or indivisible, atoms—the most solid building blocks of the world—went liquid. What had been quiet and predictable became noisy and dynamic: electrons, protons, nucleus, in some novel *relation*. These new tiny worlds within the atom clamored for explanation concerning how they themselves remained stable and cohesive.

Modern counsel on the nature of the atom must have seemed like outlandish sailors' advice (Rutherford was a farm boy from the island nation of New Zealand; Schrödinger talked about *wave* mechanics), stinking of foreign parts and science that didn't know how to take itself seriously. But what these innovators did was simple; they stopped looking for new instruments and began to look for new relationships. They were doing in the laboratory what a writer like Melville was doing in the library, the kind of thing postmodern writers find familiar—make some new use of existing reports, recycle material, regard disclosure and discovery as redistribution rather than insemination.

An easy way to explain twentieth-century innovation in the field of physics is to say that theories of electricity replaced principles of geometry. Suddenly a language of forces superseded a language of shapes, and physiological attributes once again seemed to complicate the material landscape. At large were echoes of the alchemist's bedroom talk: Rutherford's experiments showed it was no use probing forcibly into atoms: some way must be found of inducing them to speak for themselves. Niels Bohr determined that proximity affected relationships; photons were emitted or absorbed in a hydrogen atom because the electron had changed its distance from the nucleus. To understand how an electron made the transition from one of its "permitted" orbits to another (the "quantum leap"), Schrödinger and Heisenberg solved the problem by redefining its terms.

When a suitable photon was absorbed by an atom, the effect was not so much a jump across space as a retuning, a change in the pattern of its natural frequencies to a higher one. Physicists soon found themselves saying that when the atom changed its tone (absorbing the photon), it became "excited."

This new attention to relations finally gave physics and chemistry a penchant for the advances made in zoology, which had long ago abandoned the idea of the fixity of species in favor of more evolutionary models. All scientists spoke more readily of forces of attraction and repulsion, circumstance and predilection. As Emerson had insisted, "A man is a bundle of relations, a knot of roots, whose flower and fruitage is the world. His faculties refer to natures outside of him, and predict the world he is to inhabit, as the fins of the fish somehow foreshow that water exists, or the wings of an eagle presuppose air. He cannot live without a world." Design emerges in relation to situation, which is one way of explaining the moment when science becomes literature, and vice versa. With a nod to William Carlos Williams, Robert Creeley has said, "No matter what becomes of art, art is local, local to a place and to a person, or group of persons, or just what's in the air, despite how vague that sounds. It happens somewhere, not everywhere." Creeley's "local" is an acknowledgment of the material conditions of creation. Because we are not angels but subject to the laws of space, time, physicality, happenstance, influence, and desire, savvy art learns science's secret, or apprehends the truth of what Melville terms "the absolute condition of present things."

Too far in this direction, though, lies the deadly swamp of materialism. Charles Darwin needed to go down this road to highlight the problems of creationism—but he trod it warily. In his notebooks he admitted to feeling as if he devoted his life to a "fantasy." "Oh you Materialist," he mockingly berated himself in his darker moments. Materialism's mechanical intimations, its geography of step-by-step process, fouled the delicate complexity and layered depth of Darwin's webby world. Because the question *What enables a being to do what it has always been doing?* is no more "evolutionary" a question than *What enables it to do what it has never done before?* in *The Origin of Species* Darwin takes pains to complicate the orderly implications of his title;

his models branch out, create space, make finding origins and endings impossible.

By focusing his attention on sexual selection, Darwin prevented his world picture from falling into determined materialism. There is tremendous creative function in sexual selection that seems to counteract the numbers game. The fate of the losers is not death but fewer or no children. Sexual selection does not punish the weaker; it just rewards the more attractive. It has been said that sexual selection privileges the beautiful. But "attractiveness" is a more useful term, as it takes better account of the numerous forces—smells, moods, lighting, props—that determine an encounter. Sexual selection entails a mechanism that ensures difference. (What I like you may not like. What I like there may be no obvious explanation for.) It loosens the hold of material determinism and opens the door to the new. This freedom is introduced through the idea of attraction, or taste. So although the process is algorithmic, it is lived as aesthetics. Which means it is not lived like an algorithm at all. Although there are parameters for movement, there are no determinants for movement. (Aesthetics' interest in *taste*, therefore, has little to do with judgments of quality, and everything to do with preference and partiality, or the predisposition to choose one option over another.)

Still, in Darwin's model the losers die off. They are simply not attractive enough, and so their influence is thought to leave no effect on the present. But creative evolutionists insist that the present is not just the accumulated treasure of victors' traces. Embedded in its narrative is also the history of failures. We must include in our account the trace of unproductive beings, veins of fool's gold. One reason why poets such as Ian Wedde or Charles Olson have proved adept at reading Melville is because their poetics—the art of making—construct valuables in the desert. The tools of trade in traditional scholarship are designed for finding, rather than making, its treasures. Such scholarship offers a sort of archaeology of literary merit; reconstructing the shape of a thing from traces of the past has come to be what we call cultural, intellectual work. But the old adage about archaeology is true—that we are left holding those things which best stand the vagaries of time: clay, rock, metal, bone.

What we lose, along with the transient matter of paper or expression, are the affinities of motive and preoccupation.

To insist that readers of literature should be thinking not just of shapes but of forces—what *moves* you, not what *are* you— sounds hollow when positioned against the solid rock of conventional discovery. Such insights are very well, very pretty, but hardly accountable. Here cultural studies has forgotten nature. An art that tunes itself to signals outside the usual range, pays attention to forces of inclination and attraction, goes looking in unexpected places, is not some blind grope in the direction of the more precise habits of science. This art *is* science.

It is a question of changing one's frequencies. Quantum mechanics dissolved the problem of the electron's "jump" across space by reenvisioning the movement not as a jump but as a retuning, an atom's change to a higher register when absorbing a photon. Dog whistles, in other words: same parts, new tension, different reaction. And to some degree, the reaction is unpredictable—one cannot trace or witness the exact process of the call, only its response, a measurement in the shape of dogs, not the sound of whistles. Thus the abandonment of causality is in the nature of the science; for the artist, "quantum" takes the mechanical out of "quantum mechanics."

These quantum movements detail an unvisualizable process; no diagram does them justice, and it is language that finally goes the distance. Puns are perhaps a good example of being in two places at once, or being responsive on different levels, without, as it were, "jumping" or moving. The poet Jack Spicer tells the one about the guy who jumps from the twentieth-story window and the guy on the fifteenth story who looks at him falling past and yells, "You got vertigo?" And the guy who's falling yells back, "No, only about fourteen more stories." What this joke does is connect the observer in the window and the guy falling out of the window, where "vertigo" and "far to go" bring them together somehow. Dissolved is the difference between inside and outside. The multivalences of words—the voices and preoccupations of other writers and speakers, meanings that change in changing contexts, the knocking and noisy universe of expression and use—and not a word's accessible foundations, are what attach language to the world. These other mediums that try to get through on the receptive frequency of the Logos

Jack Spicer calls "low ghosts." Low ghosts open up language to its community. To be a word, a word must be receptive to these mumblings, for words, Spicer says, like poems, "cannot live alone any more than we can." Tuning in to these frequencies transforms language from a flat thing, a picture, to a scientific thing, more like a sound.

Low ghosts are the "failed" influences, the series of untraceable, or partly traceable, elements that constitute a living thing. To say that reception to these frequencies gives a text "depth" is to invoke a false picture. Better to say they give a text noise. To bring these influences into the clear light of day is to perhaps betray their use; proper archaeological survey will expose them as frauds, as somehow different from what they are thought to be. The stories of these failures are of more use at a submerged level—as Wedde says, like a mysterious, threatening reef. It is a style of paying attention to other frequencies, of hearing low ghosts, that is part of Melville's poetics. Reception to these other frequencies is maddening, however, and if one wants to avoid falling prey to the voices in one's head they must confirm, at some level, the ability to live with such a situation.

Melville's initiating low ghost is Long Ghost, who both scares and repairs. Long Ghost's frightfulness is his affirmation that yes, everything is afloat. That's the way of it. Seamen are familiar with the unanchored truth of flotsam and jetsam. What beachcombers learn quickly is that there is little to connect the layers of crap and treasure that come ashore with the tide. At sea, sailors struggle to keep clear a whole series of oppositions—real and apparent, mental and material, inner and outer, subject and object—that grow increasingly slippery the farther from shore one travels. But Long Ghost's science, his doctoring, inheres in his ability to say *so what?* It is poetic license; words are not foolproof, they may not get you where hoped—*but they will take you somewhere.* Make something up to say anyway. You can't follow a word back to its source, just like you can't follow a story to its source, but here we are in the middle of things, and somehow we have these means at our disposal. Under Long Ghost's direction, a young sailor can relax his vigilance, let the chatter in his head subside to a murmur. In a whaler, says Ishmael, "wonders soon wane":

Besides, now and then such unaccountable odds and ends of strange nations come up from the unknown nooks and ash-holes of the earth to man these floating outlaws of whalers; and the ships themselves often pick up such queer castaway creatures found tossing about the open sea on planks, bits of wreck, oars, whaleboats, canoes, blown-off Japanese junks, and what not; that Beelzebub himself might climb up the side and step down into the cabin to chat with the captain, and it would not create any unsubduable excitement in the forecastle.

After a while the sound of waves becomes a kind of silence.

The freaks, however—the failures, the poets, necks a-swivel, eyes too big for their heads—can't help but attend to the knocking in their hearts that accompanies such revelations. Their ready tendency to pun takes on an almost desperate dimension, as if they sense they must somehow make and get their own jokes. This humor is uneasy, vacillating between flippant and mournful. It insists on its ability to float along, to survive alone, even as it is always keeping an eye out for an audience, an answering wink. Such a humor or mood marks the losers. They stand out like white moths against black bark; they are unlikely to survive the trip, much less attract the crowd successful progeny calls for. Because the real nobility of the lost cause is the cry for community. To make sense there must be a sympathetic audience—at least one other coordinate to make the fact of a position real. This insistence sometimes sounds like a warning plea, echoing the fourth Percival poem in Spicer's *The Holy Grail:* "If someone doesn't fight me, I'll have to wear this armor all of my life." True failures, the most disturbing ones, cannot help but pose the question *Who will love us?* It is this need, perhaps, that makes them unattractive to a world. What's love got to do with it?

"Love" is a euphemism for the more messy forces that attract or impel, magnetize or nauseate. It is not antithetical to science but one more way to talk about the forces that shape the material world, the impulses that provoke some combined possibilities and not others. There is a certain poverty to my perception of the world that limits from range those things—dog whistles, radar—for which I have no reception. It is not that they do not exist, just that I am not tuned to them—they have no hold on me. One should see this inability not as a lack but rather as a kind of discernment, even taste. In a practical, biological sense I pay attention to that which consumes me, whether I am guest or host of the feast. All animals have within auditory range that which they can eat, and that which can eat them.

Perception measures our possible actions upon things, and also the possible actions of things on us. It is easy to think of perceptions as part of the images they represent, and as such detached from the living body. But to do so is a mistake. Perception is always organized by principles of attraction, or those motives of proximity and hunger. The creative evolutionist Henri Bergson calls these motives "affection" and says in *Matter and Memory* that we "have to take into account the fact that our body is not a mathematical point in space, that its virtual actions are complicated by, and impregnated with, real actions, or, in other words, that there is no perception without affection." One's perception of the world is entirely dependent on the conditions that affect the body—at each of its movements everything changes, like the turn of a kaleidoscope. As Bergson argues, external objects send back to a body, as would a mirror, its eventual influence; they take rank in an order corresponding to the growing or diminishing powers of the body. The objects that surround a body reflect its possible action upon them. Perception, in other words, is our version of the world in which we plan to act.

The bottom line is that we see not all of the world but only the parts that we are invested in—the parts that interest us because they have some call on our fate. Affection is what we add to objects in order to bring them into our range. Affection means the material of our perception is not distinct from us but subject to our private tastes. It means that we see what interests us. It is the condition, both private and voyeuristic, that dims the lights but advertises, like a candlelit booth, particular seductions. This aroused, attentive watchfulness is what gave science a new (literary) voice. As an Indian astrophysicist dictates in Jacob Rajin's play *The Candlestick Maker:* "Gregor Mendel . . . was a pea-brain." If you want to understand the mysteries of the physical world, he says, you need to "put your mind in a sticky place." To put it less elegantly, the world is organized by principles of attraction, the call one thing has on another. Good science, in fact, is sexy.

But of affection, of attraction, we can say nothing; we can only record the result, like so many dogs, and not the impulse. Love's greatest lesson is to prove elusive when sought out; it depends on subtler means of involvement. Though binding, the logic of love—its law—is loose. It is alchemical, not categorical. Love is ultimately responsive, so its successful strategies are solicitous, rather than determined. In a world filled with water, there is little indication that getting to the bottom of things holds any promise—an imagined dredging up of the seas, so that we may walk plainly on the ocean floor and spot whales, coral reefs, sunken hulls, at our leisure. The sea remains, which means that if one is to go fishing for its treasures, one must follow subtler means of achieving reward. We trail our lines. We sit quiet. We employ a variety of bait—dangle, sparkle, squirm, chum—and hope for a response, pray for some kind of connection.

Some fools whisper to the water, floating sweet nothings on its surface in the hope of inviting a catch. Some even offer foul encouragements, a strange kind of pornography of inducement. In *Moby Dick* Mr. Stubb, the odd blowfish, with his conical, comical, phallic cognomen, is one such queer whisperer. During a whale chase his tongue-lashings and lickings elicit from his boat crew unmatched reaction. He says "the most terrific things to his crew, in a tone so strangely compounded of fun and fury" that the fury seems "calculated merely as a spice to the fun." Stubb has not failed to miss the desperate humor of man's situation, and his dreadful delight is catching: "no oarsman could hear such queer invocations without pulling for dear life, and yet pulling for the mere joke of the thing":

> "Pull, pull, my fine hearts-alive; pull, my children; pull, my little ones," drawlingly and soothingly sighed Stubb to his crew. . . . "Easy, easy; don't be in a hurry—don't be in a hurry. Why don't you snap your oars, you rascals? Bite something, you dogs! So, so, so, then; softly, softly! That's it—that's it! long and strong. Give way there, give way! The devil fetch ye, ye ragamuffin rapscallions; ye are all asleep. Stop snoring, ye sleepers, and pull. Pull, will ye? pull, can't ye? pull, won't ye? Why in the name

of gudgeons and ginger-cakes don't ye pull?—pull and break something! pull, and start your eyes out! Here!" whipping out the sharp knife from his girdle; "every mother's son of ye draw his knife, and pull the blade between his teeth. That's it—that's it. Now ye do something; that looks like it, my steel-bits. Start her—start her, my silver-spoons! Start her, marling-spikes!"

Stubb's exhortation to his crew has about it the odor of illicit sex. But his is a practiced, practical art, and whatever its corruptions, he shows a sophisticated understanding of attraction. To Ahab's strange theater of extracted promises ("Drink and swear, ye men that man the deathful whaleboat's bow—Death to Moby Dick!") there is a response that does not participate in Starbuck's conservative capitalist fantasy ("Sperm, sperm's the play! This at least is duty; duty and profit hand in hand!") or in Ishmael's private, unpolitical musings but provides an alternative, sympathetic to Ahab, but more silly, less profound. Stubb's alchemy suggests an attention to the forces that hold us—an eye open to the socioreligious—*and* a hand in the practical matter of life. His attentions simply indicate another option, a third possibility, something fishy beneath the surface, an antediluvian element that has gone its own evolutionary way.

It is somewhat of a relief to think about the silvery bodies that did not pause to notice the Flood come down upon the earth. Also horrifying, invoking the kind of awe Ishmael feels for the "antimosaic, unsourced existence of the unspeakable terrors of the whale, which, having been before all time, must needs exist after all humane ages are over." To find a response in laughter, the strained expectation into nothing, is to make of oneself and one's own unsourced existence a kind of manageable joke. In the chapter "The Hyena," this philosophy comes clean:

> There are certain queer times and occasions in this strange mixed affair we call life when a man takes this whole universe for a vast practical joke, though the wit thereof he but dimly discerns, and more than suspects that the joke is at nobody's expense but his own. However, nothing dispirits, and nothing seems worth disputing. He bolts down all

events, all creeds, and beliefs, and persuasions, all hard things visible and invisible, never mind how knobby; as an ostrich of potent digestion gobbles down bullets and gun flints. And as for the small difficulties and wordings, prospects of sudden disaster, peril of life and limb; all these, and death itself, seem to him only sly, good-natured hits, and jolly punches in the side bestowed by the unseen and unaccountable old joker. That odd sort of wayward mood comes over a man only in some time of extreme tribulation; it comes in the very midst of his earnestness, so that what just before might have seemed to him a thing most momentous, now seems but a part of the general joke. There is nothing like the perils of whaling to breed this free and easy sort of genial, desperado philosophy.

Ultimately such species are not likely to last long. A clear eye to the cuckolding world will unseat any fantasies of future generations, and it is only the joke that is left to issue forth. Even hardy Stubb has no illusions about his influence: "Ha! ha! ha! ha! hem! Clear my throat! I've been thinking it over ever since, and that ha-ha's the final consequence":

> Why so? Because a laugh's the wisest, easiest answer to all that's queer. . . . Well Stubb, *wise* Stubb—that's my title— well, Stubb, what of it, Stubb? Here's a carcass. I know not all that may be coming, but be it what it will, I'll go to it laughing. Such a waggish leering as lurks in all your horribles! I feel funny. Fa la! Lirra, skirra! What's my juicy little pear at home doing now? Crying its eyes out?—Giving a party to the last arrived harpooners, I dare say, gay as a frigate's pennant, and so am I—fa, la! lirra, skirra!

The only progeny he can be sure to count on is this joke, this joke of a joke, which is hardly funny at all. What he does produce is some other kind of fruit. *Fruit de mer.* The balmy, salty, flippant logic that overrides the trauma of the flood (or the desperation felt by every sailor whose certainty comes unmoored). What Stubb has, like Long Ghost before him, is the knack of getting on with the business of living, even in the face of desperate circumstances: "And Stubb, fish-like, with sparkling scales, leaped up in that same golden light:—'I am Stubb, and Stubb has his history; but here Stubb takes oaths that he has always been jolly!'" This fishy philosophy has none of what Melville comes to call "earnestness" and so is still some distance from a final peace. But by equipping a seaman with the ability to swim, it provides a necessary respite between dogmatism and drowning. It should not be forgotten that this is *not* a model to emulate. Selfish, silly, perverse, Stubb is no captain and should not be followed as one. But in some sense Stubb embodies the carnal rush of terror and amusement that comes from finding oneself at a loss and being able to go on in a certain way. The fool, like a ship, is what inhabits the space between land and sea.

If the place of the fool is to tenant dual spaces, to describe this arrangement is always clumsy, like trying to explain vision using only a diagram of the retina, iris, lens. Supposing the mechanism of sight as explanatory for the evolution that called into being the creation of the eye is quietly appalling: the one is purely mechanical; the other is that awesome combination of contingency (the steps needed to construct the eye) and foresight (the answering response of material to a provocation, light, as somehow beneficial). The fool as visionary knows himself much more than the sum of his parts even while he is the victim of circumstance. Peculiarly able to see the big picture only because he pays attention to the details, he must focus, look up, focus, look up, in some human approximation of the strange ability to be in two places at once.

The fool's extraordinary ability to be familiar, to know the facts of the case, and to be generally savvy is what makes him so intolerable. What is frightening about the fool is the way he reveals that however big the world, however unimaginable its possibilities, man is still responsible for moving through it in a certain way. The fool renders intelligible the terrible condition of being afloat in the wide watery world but remaining connected to it in specific ways. In the face of all that is arbitrary, we are asked to take responsibility for what happens to us—to answer, as one would a summons, the world's expansive ambiguity. Take for instance Melville's example of the hapless Macey, who, after shouting insults and provocations to a submerged whale, experienced the kind of "accident" whose circumstances one cannot help but take personally:

The luckless mate, so full of furious life, was smitten bodily into the air, and making a long arc in his descent, fell into the sea at the distance of about fifty yards. Not a chip of the boat was harmed, nor a hair of any oarsman's head; but the mate for ever sank. (It is well to parenthesize here, that of the fatal accidents in the Sperm-whale fishery, this kind is almost as frequent as any.)

Describing this personal connection to the impersonal is one way of explaining that which is both foreseen and contingent, a lot that because of its dubious teeter between clairvoyance and calculation often falls to the fool. To quote a casual remark of Spicer's, "The fool is a kind of holy thing as well as something which is just stupid, and that's the distinction."

If all this talk of fools amounts to suggesting that as a writer Melville is tuned to different frequencies, and that these voices make his work noisy and not flat, it is also to suggest that as a philosopher Melville is aware of the possibilities of being out of tune, or not within range. That one may speak but not be heard, or that it is (amazingly) possible to speak in such a way that one is heard, are not rational convictions—consistent and coherent and repeatable—but depend, for their proof, on response. There is in fact little evidence that such interactions happen, if by evidence we indicate the means by which we can follow a certain progress. If I say to you, "Get me that pudding," there are no procedures by which I can verify that you know what I mean by "get" or "me" or "pudding," though if in fact you do bring me the pudding, then that is a kind of proof. In fact, if I am to speak at all I have not much more than my own conviction that what I have to say makes sense. The hope of attracting an answer is the hope for community.

In cases like these (in which some body says some thing to some body) there is no meaning to which I can assign a value outside the course of the appeal. There is no official gold standard with which I can *begin* an investigation, but only a kind of value that arrives as the result of an investigation. By investigation I mean the proposal to go looking for something, to be moved to look without map in territory that does not offer obvious inducement of a find. It is to put oneself in the ridiculous position of "looking" in places distinct not for their novelty but because of the presumed impossibility of their rewards. The result is more like a disclosure than a discovery—being lost in such a way as to make being found possible. Like the contents of that box known by the astonishing title "Lost and Found," odd shoes, butterfly hair clips—items entirely unremarkable in daily wear—take on a certain otherworldly glam, a hint of poetic possibility.

The peculiar position this kind of seeking puts one in cannot be settled by a claim; a claim would never come about because a "discovery" is only made by strangers. Those in the know, those attuned to such things, have no separate position from which to sing out their findings. (In the way that mountains are never discovered halfway up one, or Pacific islands are never discovered by natives. They are always seen and named from afar.) To get around in a watery world, we need measurements or coordinates. To have what we call measurements, we must agree that we are able judges of what these measurements are. This agreement is possible not because we bridge the gap that lies between us, nor because we decide to respect each other's differences in some mute bid for relativity. The first is a reasonable mechanical solution, and as a result too pedestrian; the latter is a reasonable result of putting limits on what we can know, and by all ordinary accounts not necessary. The affinities of motive and preoccupation implicate us in the world of our perception—so that it is *I* who is singled out, who finds the world turned in my direction, who feels summoned to a deliberate force. It is possible to agree on the kind of judgments we make (to speak meaningfully, for instance, in a public way) because the type of agreement indicated is not the kind one *comes to,* in the language of arrival, but the kind one finds oneself in, like finding oneself in love.

{ 3 }

THE POLITICS OF WHALE

When we examine what we should say when, what words
we should use in what situations, we are looking not
merely at words (or "meanings," whatever they may be)
but also at the realities we use the words to talk about . . .
then . . . it is plainly preferable to investigate a field
where ordinary language is rich and subtle.

—*J. L. Austin*

HOW DOES AHAB MANAGE TO USE WORDS like he means
them, so that he is not always caught in the trapping of a word
or disappointing himself by searching for its underpinning but
knows how to hunt it directly? How does he know what *whale*
means—or, what is it that saves this word *whale* from being a private thing? For the skeptic, one's whale is a private matter. Ahab
claims his whale is public—and if any two imposing schemes
endorse different judgments, then one has to hunt down the
source of the discrepancy.

Do each of us say the same things in the same situations?
Don't usages differ? As J. L. Austin has said, "people's usages do
vary, and we do talk loosely, and we do say different things apparently indifferently. But first, not nearly as much as one would
think." Ahab believes his own semantic theory, which means he
is ready to put his mind where his mouth is whenever he says
whale. This is because he sees the word *whale* not as the name
of a thing or an asserted characteristic but as the *dimension*, in
Austin's terms, *in which actions are assessed.* Whether or not this

stunt is the delusional exploit of a madman, destined to end in failure, or whether it has the makings of philosophical genius is what remains to be seen.

Say I shout from the rigging of the *Pequod*, "Whale!" By this I mean "I see a whale!" and also "Lower the boats, and away. Hurry!" and also "Kill him!" But if I shout this same word from the deck of the *Rainbow Warrior*—"Whale!"—I may mean "I see a whale!" but also "Isn't he beautiful?" Of course I can easily say that my meaning comes clear because of where I am. There is no problem in the use of this word. As Wittgenstein will come to say in *Philosophical Investigations*, "If it is asked, 'How do sentences manage to represent?'—the answer might be: 'Don't you know? You certainly see it, when you use them.'" If I worked for Greenpeace, and you thought I meant by "Whale!" "Kill him!" then this would be nonsense. In the world, the answer to "How do sentences do it?" is "Isn't it obvious?"

Where I get into trouble is when I try to explain myself. What is it that happens when I *tell* someone something? Here it looks as if my order "Whale!" must remain unexpressed, as there is always this abyss between my meaning and your understanding of it, or the order and its execution. What if I am on board a whaleboat that tries to rescue some whales by killing the handful that are diseased and contagious? Here my instruction "Whale!" might be ambiguous, so I would fortify it with encouraging gestures—the sign of shooting, gagging, or flopping around imitating pain; or perhaps stroking, murmuring, looking peaceful. But how do you really know how to recognize these signs? "Here it looks," Wittgenstein says, "as if the order were beginning to stammer." How do you know that I am not being silly, or that maybe I really am in pain? My supplemental gesture might not make my meaning clear. This gesture "*tries* to portray, but cannot do it."

Abandoned at this juncture, the game goes suddenly quiet. The silencing thing, my inability to say what it means to mean something, is the result of measuring, and then balking at, the distance between something said and something understood. What seems to be missing, when I look at the unbridgeable distance between a word and its meaning, is the basis for agreement. There appears to be a "gulf between an order and its execution." How to speak across this distance? Ahab wants to use this word *whale* in a meaningful way, which means it has to be available to the public. He must ask, as Wittgenstein will come to ask, "But how is *telling* done? When are we said to *tell* anything?" An inability to answer this question leaves one feeling that language must somehow be unfinished, or in disrepair. Not being able to respond to this question means finding an answer in silence, or finding silence a suitable answer. It entails coming to the conclusion that words might be used publicly, but that their meanings are private. If every individual has a distinct encounter with the world, but in order to speak to each other we use the same words to describe these differing experiences, it seems fair to say that the meanings of words can't be shared.

This notion—that a word's meaning is, finally, private—is the inaugural tenet of skepticism. Skepticism is often viewed as a location of extremity, a post so outside the everyday it seems almost incomprehensible, as if the skeptic must have a steady diet of disbelief to be so considered. But skeptics live among you. A skeptic is anyone for whom the possibility of connection has gone dead. These need not be world-consuming doubts; it is with words that skeptics are most concerned and curious. The basic doctrine of the neighborhood skeptic is his promise of the impossibility of one person ever *really* knowing what another person means. The reason for this doubt is evident: if I, an individual whose particular experience of the world is matchless, point out something to you, say a tree, and call it such, your encountering of the tree is bound to be different, as your understanding is different, from mine. Thus it may be said we share the term "tree" but do not share the experience *tree*. A skeptic seizes on this disjunction as proof that the meanings of words cannot be shared. What's more, the skeptic has found a kind of cultural currency among those of us who are interested in the way vocabularies legitimize hierarchies. If because I am a white middle-class Western woman, my tree is thought to be your tree, but your tree is more communal or colored by contrary investments, in the megalopolis my tree will have more clout, more capital. Apt concern over structures of authority has meant that as language users grow more aware of differing perspectives, it is less and less acceptable for us to say that different people can share the same terms. Skepticism can now be said to have morality on its side.

But what are the consequences of this alliance? If all claims to the good are circumstantial (what I call good is good for me) and not categorical, it certainly allows language users to feel let off the hook, whenever we talk about truth—or in other words, whenever we speak persuasively, whenever we speak with appeal. When I say *tree,* the culturally conscious individual says, of course I mean *my* tree. The result of this conclusion is that if you cannot understand what I mean exactly by tree, and I cannot understand what you mean, we can talk to each other, but we cannot share the meanings of words. This is a pragmatic, pluralistic stance, providing as it does the grounds for discussion and debate, if not perfect agreement. These our trees will never be the same; we will never know them, the trees of our neighbors, but we can at least share the forest.

The pluralist is rightly suspicious of sameness, which for him translates to homogeneity—a terrifying, invariable, unflinching commonality. In his fight against determinism he comes to regard shared meaning with the skeptic's eye; agreement is what we call the process of sharing differing views in a useful way. Agreement can be had in practice, but not in theory. I can agree with you over the matter of the tree, but only because what I mean by *tree* and what you mean are not the same. The pluralist hope, in effect, is that we can live in a world where we share trees but do not share the meaning of *tree.* Would that we were truly able to know what others mean—but if shared meanings entail an unshareable world, the price is too high.

Blazing like Sherman through these pretty woods is Ahab, who insists on his ability to say *whale,* to say it meaningfully, in a public way, without any attributive, qualifying adjective. His "whale" and his *whale* are the same; for him there is no distinction between saying a thing and meaning it. Is this tyranny, or is it philosophy? Assuming for the moment his right to produce the latter, Ahab's inability to distinguish "whale" from *whale* is the basis of his logic: if his philosophy is to be treated at all earnestly, this proposition must be met with sobriety.

A captain is a well-trained man. So the first thing he must do in order to accept a proposition, such as the pluralist's proposition that the meaning of a word can't be shared by different people, is to imagine a situation in which this is the case. When could a word's meaning not be shared? Well, when I say "Whale!" and you think I mean "Kill him!" when what I really mean is "Isn't he beautiful." Though it is only in quite extraordinary situations that this could happen—when I am on a whaleboat that tries to save some whales by killing others—still one must accept its possibility. But then how does this language work? Simple: when I say words there is some internal process going on by which I can distinguish between what I say and what I mean, what I *really* mean, and what I mean in certain occasions. What determines words is intention: when I use language, I am wanting words to work in a certain way.

But along these lines there is an adjustment to the world's coherence, its grammar, or stickiness, that is unsettling. Not that the world falls apart, exactly. One does not lose life; the feeling is more reminiscent of losing an article, like an article of speech—not vital but noticeably absent, like having a part of something taken, or taken off. There is a kind of legless quality to the intentional model of language that makes language's mobility questionable. One uses a word as if it were a trustworthy avenue to the experiences of others but has private reservations about its ability to go the distance.

What are the implications of saying that the way words work depends on what one wants them to do? If when I said "Whale!" I *wanted* to mean it in a certain way, surely it could then only be called luck or coincidence if two or more people happened to mean by "Whale!" the same thing as me? According to the theory that words mean according to how we want them to, language cannot help but appear inadequate—disabled, in its public distribution, by a dependence on explanatory tools that make available the meanings of words. These tools are only stand-ins for natural equipment and so they can't be counted on, which is why a skeptic or pluralist says that the safest bet is to assume the meanings of words can't be shared.

But their analysis presumes I translate words into directions for my own actions, or that I use words as signs—when I hear a word, a meaning of it goes through my mind and tells me what to do. It establishes my personal grasp of a word as a kind of definition of it. I recognize a word, go to my head for an account of it, come up with its measurement, and proceed to make meaning. But what if this account of how language works is abandoned as a model?

If Ahab can show that private ostensive definition has little to do with the way that speakers use words meaningfully, he can show that intention, or *wanting* words to work in certain ways, is not at all how language functions. When Ahab insists that there is no difference between what he says by "Whale!" and what he *means* by it, his philosophy suggests, astonishingly, that one need not worry about the cross-purposes of varying accounts of words—not because we all share the same world but because defining words to themselves is not what language users do.

Any understanding of language that relies on private definition is exasperating. As long as language use is thought to depend on private analogue, communication will fall short. Ahab's answer to the world's not knowing what he really means by *whale* is to carefully trace the difference between the idea we have of how speakers use words and the use we really make of them. He shares this interest in the employment of words with all other ordinary language philosophers, who are united in their interest in reconnecting us with words, and in their insistence that it is impossible to say something meaningfully but in the saying of it to mean something else.

Ordinary language philosophy tries to show how language is not a sport at which one plays but a world in which one works. The suggestion is that those who believe that the meanings of words can't be shared (those against whom the ordinary language philosopher must arm himself) are still searching for the meaning of a word in the word itself—as if the meaning of "whale" is in the word or the creature. According to this model what gives words their efficacy depends on what speakers want from them. Why would an ordinary language philosopher care so little for this explanation? Wittgenstein's *Philosophical Investigations* is full of experiments like the following: try reading aloud from the book you have in your hands. At the end of the page, you turn it. Once in a while you cough or mumble or look irritated on encountering a word you know to be fabricated. But how can you be sure that you are reading, and not just saying the words out loud, as if they were the words of a language unknown to you? Or what do you have to do to make this thing you are doing *reading*? Probably your first impulse is to say that the difference between speaking words out loud and reading is that in the latter case you *mean* the words to work in a certain way. According to this theory, words work only when we want them to. How fortunate! How absurd!

To prove that the meanings of words are determined not by intention but by use, Wittgenstein imagines a series of commands on a building site. The language in question consists of words such as "block," "pillar," "slab," and "beam." 'A' calls out "slab!"—'B' brings it to him. But Wittgenstein suggests that "slab!" is only a shortened form of the sentence "Bring me a slab," and so he asks:

> But why should I not on the contrary have called the sentence "Bring me a slab" a *lengthening* of the sentence "Slab!"? Because if you shout "Slab!" you really mean: "Bring me a slab."—But how do you do this: how do you *mean that* while you *say* "Slab!"? Did you say the unshortened sentence to yourself? And why should I translate the call "Slab!" into a different expression in order to say what someone means by it? And if they mean the same thing—why should I not say: "When he says 'Slab!' he means 'Slab!'"? Again, if you can mean "Bring me the slab," why should you not be able to mean "Slab!"?—But when I call "Slab!", then what I want is, *that he should bring me a slab!*—Certainly, but does "wanting this" consist in some form or other a different sentence from the one you utter?

Here it looks as though speaking even a "primitive" language depends on *wanting* words to work in a certain way. But if the evidence for how a word is used entails the user wanting to mean it in a particular way, it gives the process a kind of psychological atmosphere—which implies that "meaning it" is something in the sphere of the mind. Axiomatic to a psychological account of meaning making is the assumption that such activity is "something private," and a private means of communication, says Wittgenstein, is ludicrous—"as it were, a dream of our language."

What is the problem here? Surely it is impossible to get through the day without saying things one doesn't really mean.

But thinking that words work according to how one means them is very different from thinking about *what* one means by certain words. It is possible to say a lot about the second case, which is merely a matter of cultivation or circumstance, a question of vocabulary and intention. What words to use in order to indicate a certain meaning, or what meaning is indicated by a particular word, is something language users do often. In a court of law we might question how someone means a word ("I could have *murdered* him"), but we stop playing this game when we run out of energy or funds. It entails a kind of effort impossible to sustain in the ordinary way we use words. If I needed to determine the meaning of each word I used as I used it, I would retard and then make wretched all attempts to communicate.

If it were possible to differentiate between saying words and meaning them in a certain way, *outside of the way in which words are used,* then I should be able to say "Whale!" and *really* mean "Whale!" In fact I should be able to say "Whale!" and mean "Whale!" or even "Whale!" or better yet "Whale!" A philosopher trained in the way of the whale fishery must contend that it is possible to say "This book is really stupid" and not mean it, or not be convinced about the truth of this statement, or not be willing to say such a thing to its author: but she insists that it is *impossible* to say "This book is really stupid" and not *know what is meant* by "this," or "stupid." In the latter case there is no difference between meaning a thing and using it in a certain way. In this sense she must, like an ordinary language philosopher, admit to a kind of realism, of *knowing* what words mean, of being convinced by them.

An ordinary whale philosopher must wonder why, when in order to speak at all we must be convinced by words, philosophy is so determined to live without assurances or guarantees—why, in fact, it is criminal or negligent for a philosopher to confess and declare her convictions instead of work to rid herself of them. In order for skeptics to argue the impropriety of conviction they must use this term in extraordinary ways. But the conviction one has about the meaning of used words is nothing at all like the conviction associated with deliberate or obstinate prejudice—which would certainly make it conveniently easy to condemn. If a conviction were simply bad faith then it could always be corrected, improved, the way the wealthy like to cap their children's teeth with braces. Ignorance and intolerance and obstinacy must be corrected; this is how people hoping to live ethical lives spend their days. But philosophical conviction is *not* that which describes an individual's relation to an object or idea. It is what makes the object available to her as an object.

Let us say that Ahab is convinced by his whale. Does this mean that his relationship to it—his approach, his attitude, the varied ways in which he maintains his understanding of this thing *whale*—is beyond doubt or correction? Of course not. It simply means that he is sure that what he says, when he says "whale," is what he means. Conviction is what marks out the cohesive and flexible domain in which there are terms (and they may be changed) that we use to describe ourselves and give authenticity to our lives.

Unhappiness over the conviction that an individual's word "whale" and his understanding *whale* are the same thing originates in a pluralist's not ignoble effort to protect the world from waywardness, to better it. But the whaler, nowhere near as sure of his influence, is less winningly and more obscurely participating in an entirely different project—trying not to correct the world but to participate in it. The debate about conviction really boils down to whether a philosopher should *mean what he says*—or whether meaning what he says excludes him from the ranks of philosophy. If a philosopher's job is to speak meaningfully without really meaning what he says, then philosophy must show how one is able to do this. (Because if it is possible for someone like Ahab to show in ordinary ways that saying a thing and meaning it are inextricable, then there is other work to do.) The warning to theoretical debate from the whaling industry is that we must be wary of philosophy which, for all its linguistic genius, is thinking that hopes to say things in meaningful ways but to salvage particularity insists that what someone says is not necessarily what he means.

{ 4 }

CONFESSIONS OF A CAPTAIN

> Recognizing what we say, in the way that is relevant
> in philosophizing, is like recognizing our present
> commitments and their implications; to one person a sense
> of freedom will demand an escape from them, to another
> it will require their more total acceptance. Is it obvious that
> one of these positions must, in a given case, be right?
> —*Stanley Cavell,* Must We Mean What We Say?

IF IT IS TO BE PURSUED HONORABLY, all philosophy must begin with a confession. What might be said to get in the way of one's understanding is often not bad equipment, or missing perspicuity, but a tendency to lie to oneself about oneself. Lying to oneself distinguishes a genuine from a false style, since a reluctance to descend into one's own untidiness—because it is too hard or too painful—ensures a cursory or perfunctory treatment of the matter at hand. Lying to oneself involves underestimating the immoderate influence of one's own beliefs. A philosopher must understand belief as being equivalent to her willingness to act on a hypothesis; beliefs are the measure of connection to her world—that is, belief is what makes all claims conceivable or inconceivable to her, live or dead.

Pride, if it is the quality of refusing to concede that *wherever there is a claim there is some obligation,* is what gets in the way of genuine understanding. As Wittgenstein says of the philosopher's task, "The edifice of your pride has to be dismantled. And that is terribly hard work." But the question is this: philosophy is so bound up with self-importance that it is not clear what this hard work is—whether it is the labor of taking apart your belief structure, or the charge, *given* your beliefs, of owning up to them. In philosophy's confusion over what needs doing, "belief" has come to approximate, or equal, "pride." Prevailing wisdom imagines the work of philosophy to consist, mostly, of following this dictum: "The edifice of your *belief* has to be dismantled." Thinking of belief as a kind of structure makes plausible the project of taking it apart, or tearing it down. But some philosophers have been left wondering, how *does* one dismantle an edifice that is made up of obligations to oneself?

Call, for the moment, the decision to abandon certain attempts at dodging self-deception "having the courage of one's convictions." Is this kind of courage a blinding fantasy of conceit, or is there some genuine philosophy here? Gesturing toward the contrivances of one's faith is necessary critical work, but in some sense it is the conscientious, deconstructive business that comes *after* our most fundamental commitments, the constancies around which individuals construct and narrate their identities. Acknowledging the motivation for one's beliefs (predisposition, opportunism, dumb luck) seems the best hope of purifying them. But having previously chosen the hopeful candidates, what this evaluative procedure does is subject them to a publicity contest that the candidates by this time invite. And the most interesting show in town is the process which has already transformed these candidates into lovely contestants. Philosophy with the courage of its convictions is that which, unwilling to confuse the game, intuits the impossibility of beginning an evaluation from a place of incoherence, or outside of the guidelines that give dimension to life's events, lend focus to the venue, and create options one can in some manner vote for. This courageous, conceited philosophy simply maintains that to be in the enviable position of deliberation, one must concede, as well as introduce, various conclusions.

(The argument about the rigged quality of the choices before us has led many writers to flee the confinements of prose for the more open spaces of poetry. But even poetic parataxis, or the breaking up of the narrative pull of a sentence, does not escape these tabulated loyalties. Poetry that is politically convinced of the need to place propositions or clauses one after another, without indicating by connecting words any coordinating or subordinating relation between the clauses, announces the multidirectional, nonlinear quality of life and language. Such writing purposely avoids consecutive links—often articles like "the" and soliciting words like "therefore" and "so"—because they signify a kind of hegemony that poets don't want to vote for. But ironically poetry's removal of connecting words actually institutionalizes their sequentializing and prescriptive properties. It is poetry's removal of connecting words that betrays poetry's *belief* in these words' causal powers, and ordinary language's use of these words that reveals ordinary language's astonishment about the proposed actuality of these powers. Thus once again poetry finds itself working for free for the old order.)

A belief is shaped by contingent historical circumstance, but it is not possible to step away from our fundamental commitments far enough to see them exposed and foolish from another's perspective. Perhaps, though, this proposition is less terrifying if it is clear what is meant by "fundamental" commitments—do they include homophobia, the fear of snakes, love of all things French? What is a conviction, after all? If convictions are nothing more than a small man's small-mindedness, then he must in no uncertain terms work to slough them off. But if conviction is a quality of connection to the world, blind the way an eye is blind at the exact entrance point of the optic nerve on the retina, then the possibility does not exist for the man to stand off entirely from the viewpoint that gives sense to his world. In the first case it is feasible to handle convictions casually, to be enthralled by them but to one day discover their superficial natures, their shabby infidelities. In the second, though, conviction is inseparable from the life; proposed actions that do not accord with the conviction are puzzling, inconceivable—one is disinclined to carry them out. Most importantly these convictions cannot enjoy the freedom of incredulity; this kind of commitment essentially involves *believing* one's beliefs are objectively valid. In light of this distinction, what is the quenchless hunt for Moby Dick—can it be exchanged and bettered, or is it the immovable expression of vital action?

If philosophical conviction is uneducable because it is the unwilled, uncomprehending action of living, then we need not fear it as we fear prejudice, since it cannot survive the secret intelligence in which prejudice flourishes. Conviction, in this sense, justifies the legitimacy of a particular perspective not because one has a right to it, as it is private, but because one has an obligation to it, as it is public. Anyway what would a private conviction look like? Do you imagine it looking a little like the difference between what you mean by the word *whale* and what Ahab means? Is this "private" conviction then obscure, hooded, spectral—ferocious in the way that dreams are ferocious, latent but abandoned with the morning? Or does it "fan-tail a little curious, sir, before he goes down?" And has it "one, two, tree— oh! good many iron in him hide . . . all twiske-tee betwisk?" Is it mighty quick, and bushy, even for a parmacetty? Does it have a name? If it can be recognized and called upon, then it is in circulation. If it is in circulation, like breath, like language, it cannot be private.

It is hard not to read Ahab's hunt for the whale as a private project that has gotten out of hand, or as an attempt to make his own private way of giving meaning to his life—a romance with the magnificently opaque and uncomprehending whale— compulsory for a crew who do not share his interests. But death and devils! "It is Moby Dick ye have seen—Moby Dick—Moby Dick!" Aye, aye, Ahab shouts, "with a terrific, loud, animal sob," when it is clear that the white whale is not unfamiliar to his men: "God bless ye." If there is a word for it, it cannot be private, as words are always a public matter.

Alas, the relativist points out, there is a difference between saying Ahab's whale is private, which is easy to refute, and saying that his *whale* is private—his conviction, his reading, his assumption of what this thing means. Yes! the whaler counters, with help from ordinary language philosophy: but then are you saying that "whale" and *whale* are different things, or that what is meant by the word "whale" is not what you *mean* when you say "whale"? Are you sure that you can follow the dives and double-backing of a word that sounds in one way and means in another? Are you sure that you can follow this private whale, that you will not die in the chase?

Let's give faces to these persuasions. For Starbuck, first mate on board the *Pequod,* conviction is a willed, essentially arbitrary series of allegiances. A buyer's market. For Ahab, conviction is the inside of a lived experience. The objects of its concern are in no way derivative of particular psychological states; conviction, for the captain, cannot understand its strivings as any mere projection of habit or attitude. Who will you ship with: Starbuck, a portrait in studied sympathy, or Ahab, angrily mired in the midst of prohibitive pursuit? And is it necessary, since the decision involves committing oneself to varying but certain tragedies, to take sides?

Starbuck would say no, this is not a fixed game—but all the intelligible world is on his, angling for the best interests of their company. Ahab's desperate *yes* is an appeal for companionship, but his compulsion for rapport drives away sympathy like a parcel of rats before the rising tide. Would any ethical creature seek shelter under this single-minded captain chasing his hated fish? Starbuck's world is one of prosperity and possibility, of evenhanded justice and leveled playing fields. He is the winning dean of your child's exceptional university, the liberal intellectual, the brother you never had. Starbuck can always turn around and go home. He can change his mind. He can protect his interests, and those of his crew. Would any among you trade these colors and comforts for the ashen realty of Ahab's unerring allegiance to his nameless, inscrutable thing—that which, he declares, "commands me; that against all natural lovings and longings, I so keep pushing, and crowding, and jamming myself on all the time; recklessly making me do what in my own proper, natural heart, I durst not so much as dare?" The answer must be *yes*, a thousand times yes, if there is to be a difference between philosophy and legislation, between understanding the rules of the game and agreeing to play by the rules.

In some sense philosophy is the struggle to survive the mortification of man's allotment—our chagrin that because gaining knowledge depends on experience, the grounds for judgment are always swampy, invariably susceptible to the inducements of attachment and fixation. Ours is an awkward epistemological fate, imagined by William James in one of his immobilizing moments of panic as "a position similar to that of a set of people living on a frozen lake, surrounded by cliffs over which there is no escape, yet knowing little by little the ice is melting, and the inevitable day drawing near when the last film of it will disappear, and to be drowned ignominiously will be the human creature's portion." An impetus for all philosophizing is discomfiture; much critical study, at least, is made up of the varied attempts to safeguard humans from (or abandon us to) what feels like the precariousness of our position in the world.

James finds his footing by insisting that less ignominious than the certain disappointment of drowning is learning to swim. Enmeshed as one is in what Dewey calls the human community of causes and consequences, a syndicate as wide and deep as the world, it is simply better for man's survival to understand from the outset the manner in which he is implicated. From Jamesian resignation to this embedded fate comes our sense of pragmatism's retreat to the efficient. But while it is easy to imagine, from a postmodern climate, that in James's concession what is called "truth" melts, evaporates, or slips away from us, all James himself says is that truth is not a "stagnant property" in things but something that "happens" to things. One could say truth is still a thing, a real thing; it's just not a property *of* things. In James's philosophy, truth is no less real, no less particular, no less exclusive—no less true, in other words; it is simply the *process* that, as he says in *Pragmatism*'s lecture 6, "leads us into useful verbal and conceptual quarters as well as directly up to useful sensible termini." Truth is "an affair of leading," which is why James says that "to 'agree' in the widest sense with a reality *can only mean to be guided either straight up to it or into its surroundings, or to be put into such working touch with it as to handle either it or something connected with it better than if we disagreed.*"

Accordingly when James says "useful" we must not assume he means "helpful"—for either the cause of profit or pleasure. For James, "pragmatic" is not a stand-in for "practical." Useful means *active*, or that which does work in the world. Useful is James's name for the business an idea has with experience. Thus truth processes are useful because they "turn us *towards* direct verification; lead us into the *surroundings* of the objects they envisage; and then, if everything runs on harmoniously, we are so sure that verification is possible that we omit it, and are usually justified by all that happens." This commanding, governing quality of truth is one reason why, while "the overwhelming majority of our true ideas admit of no direct or face-to-face verification," as long as they agree with their effects and verbal expressions, they *are* true, true as "antediluvian monsters, all in their proper dates and settings." That is, Jamesian truth does not squeeze out the believer from participation in the world of sense. Truth is not capricious or elective; true ideas are neither wavering nor uncertain but in fact "lead to consistency stability and flowing human intercourse. They lead away from eccentricity and isolation, from foiled and barren thinking." Truth's duty to agree with reality should be seen in this light as belief "grounded in a perfect jungle of concrete expediencies."

However, in James's wake something has been done to pragmatism. James's interest was in what life makes of itself, his philosophy in actual fact not some happy middling between the heady rationalists and the muddy empiricists (a claim he sometimes casually makes for himself) but a practice that tries to take into account both the foreseen and the contingent, belief and experience. Pragmatism, James reminds us, "so far from keeping her eyes bent on the immediate practical foreground, as she is accused of doing, dwells just as much upon the world's remotest perspectives." But today's pragmatism has been cleansed of all spiritual leanings, its nose pressed firmly to the earth's surface.

Today's pragmatism, or more properly neopragmatism, has been reduced, expertly, to the contention that man's responsibility to find out about knowledge should be replaced with responsibility to fellow sentient beings—or that humans should stop worrying about hypothetical reason and begin to argue, to live, more reasonably. One need not consider whether a claim is valid (as all claims are destined to be shaped by the claimant's sense of their validity) but whether it conflicts with or inhibits another's claim. Within this isolated, barren realm, the pragmatist philosopher sees his role as protector—not of truth, but of the right to debate how various truths take their toll on humanity. He must become what the neopragmatist Richard Rorty calls "intellectually responsible," or accept his own obligation to justify his beliefs when his actions interfere with the actions of others. He should see this intellectual responsibility as equal to his responsibility to the people with whom he is wedded in joint venture.

Is this pragmatism America's only contribution to the field of philosophy? It is an important question on board the *Pequod,* where Starbuck's secular, representative stance seems naturally allied with an independent but united state, while Ahab's singularity invokes the old, pious, thrown-over imperial order. Ahab, clearly in slavish obedience to his convictions, fails the democratic project by not curtailing his interests when met with opposition. His is a fractious and contemptible philosophy because he refuses to dismantle the edifice of his pride—what amounts to a belief structure that has come undone from the particulars of experience.

Uncommitted in these ways, and so a better spokesperson for impartial judgment, is Starbuck: voice of reason, fiduciary of order, representative of protectorate territory. He cares for the votes of the opposition, presumably, in contrast to Ahab's unerring, unhearing disposition. Starbuck's carefulness in handling the rights of others appears to highlight Ahab's carelessness, making the captain's philosophy look sloppy and imperfect. It is Starbuck who is called by Stubb "as careful a man as you'll find anywhere in this fishery." But as Ishmael warns, "We shall ere long see what that word 'careful' precisely means when used by a man like Stubb, or almost any other whale hunter." Though Starbuck's attempt to stay uncommitted to any particular truth and so be tolerant and open-minded is the model most recently in favor in this talking America, the following chapter will begin to reveal Ahab's inability to roll over on his convictions as the philosophy most able to maintain its obligations to reason, fairness, and difference of opinion.

Indispensable to an intellectually responsible philosopher like Starbuck is his pluralism, the principle that any thoughtful question admits a variety of plausible but contrary responses. It is his pluralism that keeps the pragmatist—destined to act in his own interest—honest. Believing himself swayed by his investments, the pragmatist legislates fairness by setting up rules under which his own desires must be weighed against the desires of others. Representation and legislation are indispensable to the pragmatist because of his evaluation of the implicated nature of man's understanding.

When a pragmatist insists that statements of fact and judgments of value are the same, or the meaning of a thing is equal to its use, he runs the risk of making statements that disrupt the peace. To disable this absolute statehood ("Live free or die!" yells the Humian from New Hampshire, his reason the slave of his passions), pragmatism hitches itself to the republic. To live his pragmatism equitably, the pragmatist must quit philosophy for politics. He makes an unhappy alliance with pluralism, which, doing a disservice to both parties, finally results in an administrative and disconsolate relativism. The pragmatist, in an effort to protect the opinions of others (with whom he is not in agreement), must enlist some external force: a judge, an arbiter, a therapist, a dictionary, a lawyer, to whom he can go for, or with, evidence. Because he knows all his claims are tempered by obligation, all his facts are the products of his beliefs, his only project is to defend the rights of himself and others—particularly the right to argue. (And if you do not have a counsel for your defense, he will provide you with one.) What turns the pragmatist from a philosopher into a public servant is his conscience, which, in the profound moment of his contention that statements of fact *are* judgments of value, reveals that if the one equals the other, philosophy has lost its reason for being—or more precisely, it has lost its breath, its ability to say what is, and what isn't.

Some theorists have found a way to preserve philosophy's voice by suggesting that statements of fact and judgments of value are indistinguishable but are not the same. That is, meaning is not the same thing as use, but meaning and use are found in the same place. They are not of a perfect likeness. The queerness of the disparity between *meaning equals use* and *meaning is found in use* signals the difference between the pragmatic account of making things meaningful and this other manner of knowing, meaningfully, that things are what you make of them. But if meaning and use are indistinguishable, why not just call them the same thing? Because if fact and value are the same, then philosophy has lost the grounds of morality. A whole world of disorder opens up here. But if statements of fact and judgments of value are found in the same place but are not the same thing—or more specifically, if statements and judgments are found to depend on the same human capacities—then it is not necessary to banish the good in order to properly assess the reach and influence of value.

As long as fact and value remain the same, pragmatism allows the possibility of skepticism's favorite trick: if there is no difference between what I wish and what is, as long as there is no damning evidence for my beliefs, then the world contains no facts of which I, or someone I recognize as just, am unsupportive. Pragmatism polices the world's goods by naming them safe only when under an authorized eye—and if philosophy is to fight off the threat of skepticism it must set up rules for the existence of the world under which the "I" can wander off.

Legislative, pluralist pragmatism takes into account the tragedy of the world deaf to the cries of the one dissenting voice, but it exempts from the tragic the feeling that one's convictions can't be credited without acceptable evidence, or stand up for themselves, or count as philosophy without recourse to an external authority. The wrongness of believing without evidence, Rorty says, is the "wrongness of pretending to participate in a common project while refusing to play by the rules." The only way to be intellectually responsible is to catalog personal beliefs and submit them to the judgment of one's peers. According to this model, belief is private, truth is relative, authority is measured by degree, and commitment to a particular perspective is at best oppressive, at worst despotic. These are the rules of the pragmatist's game—and to some minds, America's game.

The most appealing aspect of this pragmatic model is its quality of discursivity. Because one does not live on the world, but in it, knowledge—everything one thinks or believes, and also everything one doubts or doesn't know what to think of—is assembled under the conditions of life. Knowing the world means having words for it; these words, though, are made coherent not by their connections to things but by the ways in which the words themselves are used. If words have a characteristic use, they have the only kind of existence they need. But the pragmatist's unhesitating concession to philosophy's inextricability from the world makes it possible for him to talk about truth rather casually, to say that what is true is what one believes—even what it would be pleasant or beneficial for one to believe. He speaks with authority but without censure because his truth is circumstantial: a pragmatist may make claim to the good (because he openly concedes that what is good is good for him), but he makes no claims to the categorical. He is unafraid to speak of truth because he wields the term with the nonchalance of one who only leases but does not buy—the ease of one who wears his opinions loosely, as if they are borrowed clothes.

There is, in this vein, a generosity and sense of courtesy to pragmatic pluralism that Ahab's philosophy does not possess. The pragmatist acknowledges his partiality in so graceful a gesture one almost forgets where he put it. To the rock of objectivity the relativizing philosopher will not cling, but he will airily invoke its *ideal* when his environment encourages him to be a partisan. Like the best kind of statesman, he would never deny his own preferences, when asked, but these affinities do not blind him to the persuasions, and particularly the contributions, of others. Next to him, the philosopher who, for lack of a better term, has the courage of her convictions, or who does not pause, or pretend to pause, to place a charitable "I think" before she speaks, or to say, "I believe I am right, but of course this belief is the product of innumerable forces to which I cannot speak or point but which I *remember*, and though these affinities may shape my every purpose and interest, they would never dissuade me from some alternative view"—next to the open-minded pragmatist, this philosopher appears sweaty and dogmatic, delusional, shoddy, inappropriate, and vain.

Ahab's most famous characteristic is his conviction. Conviction translates, reasonably enough, as arrogance—even, on occasion, as tyranny. But is Ahab's conviction really bartered for magnanimity and sophistication? He refuses to deconstruct his commitment to what Starbuck calls "vengeance on a dumb brute," lending his philosophy a kind of monomaniacal resolve. *Commitment* seems the deciding factor between these two men's philosophies. If Ahab is identifiable by his singular purpose, his scarred resolution, Starbuck is elastic, yielding: "His pure tight skin was an excellent fit; and closely wrapped up in it, and embalmed with inner health and strength, like revivified Egyptian, this Starbuck seemed prepared to endure for long ages, and to endure always, as now; for be it Polar snow or torrid sun, like a patient chronometer, his interior vitality was warranted to do well in all climates."

Like adjusting to the weather, like changing a mood, Starbuck can shift and redirect his desire to hunt whales. So, unlike his captain, the first mate is no crusader after perils: "In him courage was not a sentiment; but a thing simply useful." In Starbuck's business of whaling, "courage was one of the great staple outfits of the ship, like her beef and her bread, and not to be foolishly wasted," and so Starbuck is not to be found lowering for whales after sundown, or "persisting in fighting a fish that too much persisted in fighting him." For, thinks Starbuck, "I am here in this critical ocean to kill whales for my living, and not to be killed by them for theirs." According to the relativizing first mate, commitment is threatened by vulnerability or disadvantage—and it is right that it should be so. Commitment sinks a ship. Skin can't stretch to cover conviction. This natural disinclination to overstep the bounds of one's contract makes the first mate a good statesman, but perhaps it is not the kind of philosophy that outlasts a lifetime.

If one is to take Ahab seriously as a philosopher, or if his conviction is to be taken seriously, it must be possible to prove that holding a belief tightly enough to be called a conviction is difficult or can be called hard work. Also that having a conviction does not outlaw the possibility of freedom, or difference— because if one is to argue for the appropriateness of convictions, they must be useful to the kind of world in which one hopes to live. (Which means that having embraced a particular perspective, or having been, without nonchalance, in the grip of it, it must be feasible to experience something new. *How* this is possible requires solicitous consideration, which we will give it—but what must suffice for now is that relativity is *in itself* no obstacle to certainty.) If Ahab is to be termed a philosopher, it must be clear just what his conviction means.

The pragmatic pluralist or relativist saves himself from drowning ignominiously by refusing to commit—to a particular position, to the meaning of a word, to the prospect of the real. But commitment is Ahab's staple, his beef and bread. Say I call this other, dubious philosophy "cetologism," invoking Wittgenstein's logical investigation of discursivity and Melville's controversial exploration of cetology. There is a blush of moral realism to cetological philosophy that to a sensitive eye has the smell of something fishy *[sic]*, an overly zealous, or too ardent—even fanatical—quality that is not unembarrassing to embrace. It is so much nicer to be on the other side. Pragmatism's aim is to accept the philosopher's involvement in the world (his inclinations, his unavoidable preferences) while legislating to accommodate the richness and diversity of different perspectives. To sustain this position, the gentleman pragmatist waives his right to the truth at each new confrontation with contesting views (or so he hopes, or so he says) and so remains, he suggests, tolerant and broad-minded.

On the other hand the cetological philosopher is no less aware that her truths are circumstantial, that what feels natural and conclusive is nothing more than what has happened to come ashore with the tide. But she refuses to pretend that she can somehow shrug off these convictions when they become a liability. *Of course* her truth is fashioned, not found; the cetologist knows that things are what you make of them. But she is unwilling or unable to then perform the ventriloquism required for participation in the claim that she does not find these truths *real*.

The story that forms her understanding must be coherent, which means she cannot hold, in her mind, competing stories. (The irreconcilability of more than one story does not preclude different options but does preclude incompatible versions of reality's candidates. The difference, for instance, between the deliberative "Do I admire my successful mother or do I resent her?" and the discrepant "Do I believe my mother is a human or do I believe my mother is a robot dressed to look and smell human?") The pragmatist talks as if he thinks he is right but also as if he knows he is not right. But how can thinking and knowing be different, the cetologist wonders? How can they not be in the same place, or how is it that she could hope to speak from these two dissimilar places at once?

The cetologist's inability to differentiate between thinking a thing and knowing it, or saying one thing and meaning another, suggests the impossibility of her not meaning what she says. Thus when she talks about truth she does not say, "This is true," and *mean* "This is true *for me*," the way a careful pragmatist suggests she must. She says, and means, that what is true for her is true for all men. Can she possibly mean this? Can she live with herself, saying that her truth is not private, but public? (Can the pragmatist live without himself, when he claims that he is not convinced by what he means?) Is truth finally private, as the pragmatist suggests, or is it public, the cetologist's conviction? Or rather, how is the populace best served: by the pluralist-pragmatic pledge to protect the individual's right to his own version of truth by encoding belief as a private project—or by the cetologist's promise that beliefs are always spun from the fabric of the community, making the existence of a private conviction impossible?

Every philosopher wants to be open to revision, to be able to correct herself when her argument is clumsy or inadequate or harmful, so it is simple to acknowledge as courageous, but reject as tyrannical, those in whose grip truth is less congenially relinquished than in the cool hands of the pragmatist. Who would not fight to destroy infallibility or prefer a world of competing voices in which the most cherished opinions could be dragged to the bar? But the question on the table is this: does the cetologist's ungentle subjectivity, her dogged determination to mean what she says, really omit the possibility of difference? Perhaps the conviction that one's truths are true sounds like a recipe for tyranny only because it is thought that having a conviction is effortless, self-serving. It would appear as though there is nothing as convenient as thinking that what is true for oneself is true for everyone. But how convenient is a conviction, after all? A conviction is thorough in a way that an inclination is not. It is ever-present, uncanny, consuming. It is partial to such an extreme extent that it begins to look impartial—made seemly, like a sore cleaned by maggots, as the result of reveling in, and not transcending, its own dirty business.

Where the pragmatist and cetologist begin to offend each other is in the matter of style. To the statesman philosopher, the cetologist's convictions are so clearly her own that they are made untrustworthy. To the cetologist, freshly arrived on shore, the pragmatist's promise that he will attend to and heed that which will appear outlandish to him sounds disingenuous. There is an offhandedness to the pragmatic solution that makes the cetologist uncomfortable (as he is repelled by how hard she works to arrive, harassed and tormented, at similar findings). To protect the voices of others, pragmatist philosophy contends that one's convictions cannot be credited without evidence or stand up for themselves—which is like saying they don't count as philosophy—without recourse to the authority of the community. The wrongness of believing without evidence is the wrongness of pretending to participate in a common project while refusing to play by the rules.

But what are these rules? The cetologist counters that since belief is inherently a public project, thinking to submit it to the judgment of peers is to play the game backwards. How ridiculous, she says, to think to bring before the jury the very body that elected them in the first place and ask that its value be investigated. The cetologist comprehends the motivation for a pragmatist's bluff—to seem less of a freak—but calls this need a kind of therapy, not philosophy. Let us be clear about what a conviction is: a conviction cannot be judged because there is nowhere to stand outside of it—it is what's meant by the criteria for judgment.

The cetologist is interested in, even fascinated by, the certainty, in Wittgenstein's phrase, that to make statements, humans must be able to share not only definitions but judgments—which suggests that conviction is the public matter that *precedes* inspection. Philosophy that does not underestimate what it is to have a conviction, or that does not use the term provisionally or in a makeshift manner, understands "conviction" as tantamount to the way in which a community, in order to understand itself, must share judgments. Philosophy of this kind says there is no way to not have this shared understanding before critical determining—which means that a judgment cannot somehow incorporate a neutral statement that does not itself imply a trajectory of action.

A lawyer, a pluralist, or a relativist might say that there are actions and then there are judgments, whereas a cetologist argues (less convincingly) that judgments *are* actions. Commitments must precede intention because it is commitment that gives life meaning—not, after the fact, evaluation. Unlike assessment, conviction does not report facts but makes them recognizable; conviction is what gives things their shape. What I am convinced of depends not on what I think about the world but on the way the world is. And this inability to be indifferent to the world's matter (to why a thing matters) is something cetology thinks we have to investigate, rather than rage against or charge with the offense of turning what might be into the prison sentence of what must be.

Why philosophies of action so instantaneously raise hackles is because they elicit the question of how conviction can be ethical. If conviction equals unhesitating activity, what happens when a conviction is wrong? There must be some thoughtful measure that forces the individual to pause, to evaluate an action before it causes damage. The hardest thing a cetologist must say, and it is the thing for which she is condemned, is the following: *a conviction is never wrong.* This is because the conviction we are talking about is not the willful acting out of an individual's private prejudice—there is no "willing" involved. Moral philosophers who are swayed by the science of commitment often protect their sympathies by suggesting that of course *some* convictions may be mistaken, and these cases must be ferreted out. But if conviction is to have any ethical meaning at all, it must be defined by its infallibility. These are terrifying terms. But more frightening to a cetologist is the conflation of conviction and oppression. If conviction is understood as a word for private interests, then the world is full of false convictions. Pointed out in this context is the "conviction" of the Nazi or Klan member, the homophobe, the imperialist, the zealot. But a cetologist denies the authority of conviction to these closet opinions. How is this not, assuming the cetologist can gracefully explain what she does mean by a conviction, a stupid semantic game? Why is she willing to risk her reputation over a debate about these provisions?

A cetologist's job is to get to the heart of the matter. A "wrong conviction" would be one that, when thrown into the general arena, feels unsound or inconceivable to some members of the public. When people guilty of such an opinion defend their perspective, we say that their grip on truth is flimsy or inadequate—that they are grasping at straws. One term for this belittled opinion is prejudice, and it is usually designated by its implausibility for some portion of a community. It is conceivable how prejudice, which curtails an individual's perspective and blunts or abbreviates a person's ability to see something, may be taken for conviction—both are attributes that mark out or delimit the picture before one. But it is essential to distinguish between the two, or find them different not just in degree but in kind.

Prejudice always has a defense, even if it is irrational or implausible, even if it is only "Well, I just think that way, and I have a right to my opinions." Conviction, on the other hand, makes no appeal for confirmation. It does not in any way call for evidence. With conviction, there is no question of recourse to an external authority; one need not supply again what is already there. Because conviction takes care of itself, it is less dependent than prejudice on its hosting organism—it doesn't need to make itself likable in any regard. Under the sway of prejudice, one wants something to be so because one believes or suspects that it is so. But in the thick of conviction, one is sure that something must really be so, whether or not one *wants* it to be. Thus follows an important distinction: prejudice is a convention shaped by convenience—it will never make one's own life more difficult to believe such and such, but easier, simpler, smaller. Conviction, on the other hand, is often unhappily inconvenient. This troublesomeness gives conviction a kind of legitimacy that prejudice does not have.

Conviction is the whole package; it shows us what we want to see and also what we don't. It is disadvantageous, inopportune— not necessarily looking out for our best interests, but simply making things known or meaningful. Conviction is what makes something coherent. It is the domain in which things are perceived and as such does not depend for its truth on a particular view but is open on all sides. If conviction is said to equal prejudice, what Sartre calls a fundamental gesture of bad faith, then it would be antithetical to that quality of intelligibility that, accommodating each and every opposition, occasions the coherent. The endowment of coherence is, surely, to support all facts hung upon it. Conviction neither accepts nor asks for evidence because it has, a priori, an alibi for every interrogation, an impunity for each accusation. Prejudice, on the other hand, prays for validation. It relies on corroboration, even if this reliance means going without it, or flying in the face of it—prejudice's "evidence" need not in any way be evident. While it is possible to defend one's prejudices (even if this entails refusing to), the only response, when one's convictions are questioned, is absolute bafflement. An expression of speechless and wrenched stupefaction. The danger, then, of confusing conviction with prejudice is that it lends prejudice the coherence that is conviction's alone; it gives authority to the opinion that there is a kind of sense to prejudice's violences of the imagination.

Is it not obvious that a conviction is so hard to live by that it provides its own censure, more rigorous and punishing than any mindful judge could ever hope to produce? As unflinching support and thoughtless activity, a conviction does not rest, or pause, or make room for disagreement, or habituate, or pretend. It can't be reasoned with, or intimidated, or bought, or offended; it will never be persuaded. A conviction does not come out of its study for lunch. In the chamber of one's most secret intimacies a conviction takes on a public persona. A conviction is not a stand-in; it is not a part that somehow hopes to represent the whole; it is not an extract—squeeze conviction from a life, *and there is no remainder.* Quarantine a conviction, and it vanishes—a conviction cannot live alone any more than we can. The cetologist guarantees that loosening one's grip on a conviction is neither possible nor desirable as an ideal. This is so because people are inconsistent, but convictions are not. The more prudent the conviction, the more scrupulously it is scaled down to a tenet, a confidence, a persuasion, a bent, a proclivity, a surmise, a fondness, the harder it is to hold it accountable. Having a conviction is not easy. A conviction is mammoth, more immense than any person can imagine—obsession is too small a word for it. It is that which makes sense of *everything* else. Unless a conviction is a life, it is a lie.

But what does this mean about the possibilities of freedom: are we doomed to follow our convictions until they kill us—or is there some other way to interpret the license found under indebtedness? Perhaps conviction is less conservative than it seems, if it does indeed indicate a dimension in which actions are assessed. The pragmatic-pluralist promises to increase the broadness of his mind by narrowing or diminishing the result of his own particular tastes, but the cetologist, feeling the strain and cramp of trying to minimize herself down to an unimposing wraith, starts to wonder about the advantage of reduction. She rethinks the conditions of largesse. And she also, from an entirely different direction, comes to the conclusion that size does matter.

Anyone who hopes to live in an ethical world must consider the question of how it is possible to accommodate the demands of those with whom one is in opposition or disagreement. One must grapple with the problem of how to attend to the claims of others while recognizing there will be some claims to which we are attuned, and some to which we are deaf. The responses to this problem tend to fall into two disparate camps: the one, well funded, charitable, popular, and supported by the intelligent and humane commitments of private liberal arts universities around the country, suggests that the best way to handle the problem of otherness is by admitting the relativity of truth, de-naturalizing one's own doctrines, increasing diversity through representation, remembering to say who you are and where you come from before making an association, and on each and every occasion speaking not from conviction but from the margins of possibility. The expectancy of these benevolent professionals is to grow so small that one's influences and preferences cast no shadow. (Here one may never be too rich or too thin.)

Those on the other side, whose rhetoric happens to particularly attract the autocrats, the homophobes, and the mono-maniacs, who are mocked and disparaged (often rightfully); who are customarily awkward, ungainly, disheveled, and uneducated; and in which group the cetologist, and this writer, must find themselves, do not accept the isolation of a recognizable malfunction as the appropriate system for studying and trying to correct it. They find pathological the project that tries to narrow down appropriate approach in order to make available the suitable grounds for a critique. What is called a "recognition" of difference depends in part on analysis and collation, because to recognize something the rational intellectual must first identify it. Identification segregates and confines the wandering and spreading quality of the discursive process. Identification implies that the recognition of a thing comes *before* the recognition of all things with which it is in community. The answer to the question of accommodation, in this camp, is that the best way to preserve difference is by getting bigger.

Believing there is no way to dismantle the edifice made up of obligations to oneself, the cetologist stops attempting to do so. Instead of making room for different perspectives by trying *not* to be herself, she finds, to her surprise, that the more she is herself, the more of herself there is, the better the chance others have of being themselves. In other words, the more she is she, the more they are they. This is because theirs are not competing accounts. The one does not displace the other, as if they were parts in some economist's pie. They are connected in such a way that the prosperity of the one suggests a reciprocal, umbilical prosperity of the other. The cetologist finds that the more true she is to her truths, the better she serves the truths of another—not because what is true for her *applies* to them, but because the *trueness* of her truths vindicates and endorses the trueness of their truths. What opportunity there is in being oneself.

The pluralist bucks at the outrageousness of so categorical a decree, but to make good on his own discrete alternative, he must show how he can escape the participant perspective. He must show how it is he sees his own objects (his two hands, his mother) as having only derivative value, resulting from the projections of a certain efficacy. To preserve the truth of the many, he must sacrifice his own truth, the truth of personal investment. For him, finally, for something to matter (or count as true), it must be viewed independently from his own deep interest. Were the cetologist to grant the possibility of this floating, disembodied, unindentured position, however, there still needs to be written into the pragmatic, pluralist account some means by which the will may decide which objects it engages as important. That is, according to the relativist, the will freely alights on its objects of interest—it comes to them from an external position, in a mood of discovery. But unfettered by investment, how does the will know the field of its deliberation? What gives the world of the relativist coherence? How does this disengaged will know which concerns to weigh and test, or what, of all ponderable possibilities, to scrutinize?

What is controversial here is the claim that there is no alternative to the fact of one's convictions—Ahab's claim. Relativism's pet Starbuck says there is, and he calls this ability free will. On board the *Pequod,* these differences play out in Ahab's sense that he must pursue the whale, and Starbuck's understanding that Ahab has the authority to choose not to, if he so wishes. The first mate's message appears to be "Captain Ahab: at any moment (save the last) you can abandon this mad pursuit and choose to go home":

> Oh, my Captain! my Captain! noble soul! grand old heart, after all! why should anyone give chase to that hated fish! Away with me! let us fly these deadly waters! let us home! Wife and child, too, are Starbuck's—wife and child of his

brotherly, sisterly, playfellow youth; even as thine, sir, are the wife and child of thy loving, longing, paternal old age! Away! let us away!—this instant let me alter the course! How cheerily, how hilariously, O my Captain, would we bowl on our way to see old Nantucket again! I think, sir, they have some such mild blue days, even as this, in Nantucket.

The freedom Starbuck offers is choice. Were this whale chase led by Starbuck, a whaler would be able to turn away from, to not see, the thing in which his investments are sunk—that which employs him and to which he is committed. At first glance Ahab appears the illogical one, when he cannot seem to heed Starbuck's rational appeal. Who is not convinced by Starbuck's campaign? But before you shop here, you should know that though all the available options look as if they accommodate different tastes, the selection has been limited.

It is hard to avoid following Starbuck's lead, thinking along the lines of constructing a picture we could make but then not use. But isn't the first mate's advice something like erecting a sign that reads "Disregard This Sign"? As Wittgenstein will come to warn the would-be pluralist, concerning this straw man, "I can look for him when he is not there, but not hang him when he is not there." Starbuck still thinks it is possible to turn away from matter as if the objects of our interest and affection have no call on us, as if we could see them without being implicated in our vision. But because we can never know anything for which we have no use, apprehending matter *means* having it mean something. The great difficulty is not to represent the whale's chase as if it were something one couldn't do. As if there really were a whale, from which one gets a description, but from whose summons one is immune. But the captain's point is that there are no objects derivative or unequal to their conception. The one thing that this whale cannot effect, for Ahab, is the kind of satisfaction to be had from the cognizance of a projected state.

Of course the *Pequod* could turn around and head back to Nantucket. But this would be no solution to Ahab's problems— a man bowed and humped as though he were "Adam, staggering beneath the piled centuries since Paradise." Ahab is not a man acting in accord with his own will; he feels as if he is ordered, as if he trails blindly the thing that pulls at him. With Starbuck he is honest about this powerlessness. It is a "nameless, inscrutable" thing that commands him, that he keeps pushing and crowding and jamming himself on all the time. Does Starbuck think that he *chooses* to chase this whale? Starbuck, says Ahab, should pay better attention. This is not Ahab's private concern but a planetary one: "Look! see yon Albacore! who put it into him to chase and fang that flying fish? Where do murderers go, man! Who's to doom, when the judge himself is dragged to the bar?"

Starbuck's obvious assumption is that herein lies the distinction between man and the animals—will. In his mind Starbuck represents that willed creature, man, while Ahab is motivated by an animal force. But how does Starbuck understand this action of willing? Why is it a misunderstanding? Willing, Wittgenstein will say, "if it is not to be a sort of wishing, must be the action itself. It cannot be allowed to stop anywhere short of the action." The logic here is elegant. For example, can I will myself to speak but not speak? Yes, but then I am willing myself to not speak. Can I speak, without willing it? Who can say? Only if I suddenly lost my voice, I wanted to speak but found it was impossible, would it make sense to say that I willed myself to speak but couldn't. In this case one can say, with Wittgenstein, "I will, but my body does not obey me." One cannot say, with Augustine, "My will does not obey me."

Willing is not a tool by which I get the job done: "When I raise my arm" says Wittgenstein, "I do not use any instrument to bring the movement about. My wish is not an instrument either." The willing is the job: "Let us not forget . . . when I raise my arm, my arm goes up. And the problem arises: what is left over if I subtract the fact that my arm goes up from the fact that I raise my arm?" Nothing is left over, which means that the action must equal the willing. Willing cannot be divorced from the doing, which suggests that if man defines himself by his ability to will alone, he is in trouble of losing the basis of his distinction. As the captain cries out, "Is Ahab, Ahab? Is it I, God, or who, that lifts this arm?"

To make matters both more and less complicated, if willing is action, then as Wittgenstein says, "it is so in the ordinary sense of the word; so it is speaking, writing, walking, lifting a thing, imagining something. But it is also trying, attempting, making an effort." In other words willing is doing something *but also not doing it*. Willing is what you are doing or not doing. Willing is whatever action you take. Starbuck thinks Ahab chases the whale because that is what he wills, but Ahab knows that "willing" to chase the whale or "willing" to go home amounts to the same thing. This small chapter sounding out Starbuck's last testament to the world he wants—clear, lucid, intelligible—is called "The Symphony." The will is not instrumental to how one lives one's life; the will is how one lives one's life. Commanding Ahab to stop looking for the white whale is like telling anyone else, "Don't think about white elephants." The brain simply does not process this direction. It has nowhere to go except where it was commanded not to go.

To say that Ahab is convinced about his need to chase the whale is to say that for him this action has ceased to become a willed activity. Like thought he flies to the object under attention and cannot let it go. Is it wrong to defend conviction thus—or more precisely, is conviction wrongly defended as the practice of the proud, the tyrannous, and the determined? To see his quest for the whale as Starbuck sees it, Ahab would have to be prepared to suppose that his desire could just as well have alighted on any other creature. *But Ahab is a whaler.* To see his object from some extraterrestrial place and know that he and not the fates has made it his is a feat he is incapable of—and this is not his idiosyncrasy but man's. Any thing is what it is only through everything else. And Ahab's everything else is such that this whale and he are not disparate parts of incommensurate games but related pieces of the same game.

Starbuck thinks to unclench conviction with explanation, but his reason is forever subordinate to his captain's attunement:

"Great God! but for one single instant show thyself," cried Starbuck; "never, never wilt thou capture him, old man—in Jesus' name no more of this, that's worse than devil's madness. Two days chased; thy very leg once more snatched from under thee; thy evil shadow gone—all good angels mobbing thee with warnings: what more wouldst thou have?—Shall we keep chasing this murderous fish till he swamps the last man? Shall we be dragged by him to the bottom of the sea? Shall we be towed by him to the infernal world? Oh, oh,—impiety and blasphemy to hunt him more!"

But Ahab can be no plainer about the texture of a philosophical conviction: that it does not have the feeling of a private, volitional act. That it cannot be examined, submitted to scrutiny. That it is uneducable, immune to correction:

> Starbuck, of late I've felt strangely moved to thee . . . But in this matter of the whale, be the front of thy face to me as the palm of this hand—a lipless, unfeatured blank. Ahab is forever Ahab, man. . . . Fool! I am the Fates' lieutenant; I act under orders. Look thou, underling! that thou obeyest mine.—stand round me men. Ye see an old man cut down to the stump; leaning on a shivered lance; propped up on a lonely foot. 'Tis Ahab—his body's part; but Ahab's soul's a centipede, that moves upon a hundred legs. I feel strained, half stranded, as ropes that tow dismasted frigates in a gale; and I may look so. But ere I break, ye'll hear me crack; and till ye hear *that*, know that Ahab's hawser tows his purpose yet.

Starbuck wants his captain to "show himself," by which the mate means make himself free from all affinities and preoccupations—just as the landlubber in search of a precise picture hopes the whale will show himself, rising above the water to stand like an elephant for his portrait. But being alive means participating in a mess of innumerable legs and lines (centipedal, not centripetal), an entanglement of passions and projections. Ahab's scornful response to Starbuck, and it is not without affection, is to insist that if Starbuck could only get clear about how thick and unstable this contingency is, he would be less embarrassed by excess, or the strange commitment to tow one's purpose with half the witless instruments of reckoning flailing in the wind.

In his heart, Ahab glimpses his affliction, namely, "all my means are sane, my motive and my object mad"—but knows himself unable to divorce his object, or end, from his method of knowing it. His sworn enmity to the whale might be lacking principled rationale, but he is "without the power to kill, or change, or shun the fact; he likewise knew that to mankind he did long dissemble; in some sort, did still. But that thing of his dissembling was only subject to his perceptibility, not to his will determinate." In this matter of unprincipled behavior, Ahab is less guilty of infraction than the conniving men who sent him—a living instrument in whom this special lunacy stormed—to sea. As Ishmael tells it, after the captain's first violent encounter with Moby Dick, his furious brooding made him more appealing, not less, to his Nantucket owners: "Nor is it so very unlikely, that far from distrusting his fitness for another whaling voyage, on account of such dark symptoms, the calculating people of that isle were inclined to harbor the conceit, that for those very reasons he was all the better qualified and set on edge, for a pursuit so full of rage and wildness as the bloody hunt of whales."

Ahab's distinguishing, luckless skill is to guess the difference between choosing the terms of one's existence and understanding how one got those terms. He knows life's most secret intelligence is not what a thing *is* but how it connects to all other things, how he connects to all other things. Connection is never linear and progressional, but arterial, webby; it tentacles outward in inextricable disorder. To include the concerns of an entire life, the link from man to matter must be pursued backward and outward, externally and internally. When Ahab refuses to pull himself out of relation with the whale, he is enacting his categorical imperative, his golden rule: *no appetitive state can see its own object as having only conditional value.* More mortal than programmatic, though, the captain publicizes his vision in very human ways. Instead of acting as though the maxim of his action were by his will to become a universal law of nature, Ahab, with disconcerting valor, acts as though the universal law of nature were, by his action, to become his will.

{ 5 }

CROSSING THE LINE

To do philosophy is to explore one's own temperament,
and yet at the same time to attempt to discover the truth.
—*Iris Murdoch*, The Sovereignty of Good

STARBUCK, SURE OF HIS OWN BRAND OF AFFECTION,
thinks his captain antipathetic, unyielding, unconcerned with
public opinion. But when Ahab insists his attachment to the
whale is not the willed investment of a signatory but the involuntary instrumentality of a participant, he underscores human
involvement in its own narrative. Ahab eschews the precious
image of man as a detached observer and recognizes himself
as one thing among many floating in an unpredictable sea. He
knows his buoyancy is dependent on circumstance; that he may
at any moment go down; that his health and happiness are ten-
tative and conditional; that he is at each elbow wedded to the
fate of those things that neighbor him. It is this susceptibility to
influence that makes Ahab's position, for all its bloody belliger-
ence, more tuned to the desires of those whose company he
keeps than that of his capitalist associate.

Starbuck's wisdom is cold and to that extent stupid. But
Ahab's difficult, maddening, uncompromising substitution of
ability for *willingness* in belief's measurement changes a private
treatise about theoretical interests into a public contract based
on association and response. Although Ahab is often accused
of blind, driving ambition and alienating paranoia, of having
a rude and undemocratic outsider's plan, his search for the

whale is never out of accord with the interests of those with whom he shares a history. Ahab corporealizes knowledge, or refuses to see himself as a mathematical point in space; his is a body open to the effect of other bodies. Which means, comfortingly, that his examples aren't fixed, or that under his leadership one does not have to settle for the predictable or formulaic, the heterosexual, corporate, cultivated versions of the democratic project. Ahab's conclusions are not determined because his outlook is always open to the living influence of its findings; in the moment of confrontation a whaler is thrown against some dissimilar, animate surface—whose convulsions and spasms are not unaffecting. Cetological encounters cannot happen in isolation, and as is the case with all meetings between two or more vital forces, the interaction is heavy with the prospect of unanticipated possibilities.

But Ahab also goes one step further: the captain sees himself not simply as an object moving among other objects, unthinkingly responsive to their physical influence, but as *human*, vulnerable to emotional states. That is, Ahab can be knocked about, damaged, aroused; but he can also be resentful, embarrassed, sympathetic. He can scheme, prevaricate, imagine any number of possible futures, wait for a bargain, be impressed. His brand of philosophy is not associated with an isolated, unrealistic conception of will but is fully inhabited. Which means, in the simplest sense, that he has not disregarded reality's effect on his person (his missing leg proves the world's intrusion!) or his effect on *it*—he knows his impression of the world informs and decides his lot. This mutual impressionability, this human exchange of affections and grievances with worldly substance, is what signals Ahab's romantic nature.

What marks *Moby Dick* as a great American love story is its genius for showing that what holds a man and his world together is more gummy than luck or legality, and it is this symbiotic property that Starbuck's recital of Ahab's mad pursuit fails to make sense of—the *stickiness* of cognition, the mutually constitutive, reciprocally transformative union of mind and matter. We are speaking here of the impossibility of disinterested association—the reason why any study of the method and limits of knowledge must never forget knowledge's debt to the amatory and libidinous. Love is interesting insofar as it admits an understanding unavailable to the nonlover, and as such it is an invaluable tool of perception. Without affection there is no perception. Affection is what we add to objects in order to bring them into our range—what makes some things sensible or significant. It is the adhesive quality that joins us to the objects of our interest and brings those objects (through a guaranteed involvement in their constitution) *near* to us. Nearness to things is dependent upon man's propensity for making sense of them. One of the lessons of the whaling industry is that without a notion of what should be done with them, those things we encounter in the world remain indistinct, incomprehensible—so conceptually loose and disorganized they are not yet things. Describing phenomena along these lines is like saying they are at one time "objects" of vision as well as "ideas." Here perception is not the detection of something discoverable in nature, or the disclosure of private imaginings, but an impression created in the course of life and brought to nature as a measure of the possible. The world needs attention to configure itself, and as Ahab insists, this attention is not suddenly called upon for ceremonious occasions but is constant, dogged, enduring.

So why is Melville's love story so rarely understood as one? Because a decorous, routinely approved reading cites Ahab's whale-hunting obsession as a wanton, illogical act. Imagining his hunt for the whale as a kind of gratuitous violence and groundless hostility, this reading dismisses Ahab's commitment and desperation as outlandish, inexplicable—something of which one wants no part. It entails seeing Ahab as an alien, perverse and incomprehensible.

But to declare a thing incomprehensible is to kill it before we know what its possibilities are. It is to equate the foreign with the unaccountable, and unaccountability with offense. A more custodial readership worries about what happens when we do *not* keep Ahab within our confidences but agree to expose him as a pervert, a criminal. Those convinced of the intelligibility of Ahab's actions imagine his quest as a kind of promise. His pursuit of Moby Dick guarantees that there are certain assemblies of people (Ahab calls them crews) who, when grouped around a common object, like a whale, have recognizable dealings with that object. In these cases, the object in question is considered "interpretable," even if the object is not given to rhetorical flourishes. Moby Dick is Ahab's interpretable object. Which means Ahab's proposition—that he understands the significance of this whale, or knows what to do with it—is not unprincipled, but readerly.

In other words, it seems fair to say that Ahab's reading of Moby Dick is wrong—forced or affected—but not that the act of reading Moby Dick is wrong. And isn't that what causes consternation—the sense that Ahab is not entitled to make meaningful his experience with the whale? That since Ahab himself is not Moby Dick, nor is he privy to everyone else's encounter with Moby Dick, he cannot with any justice or certainty say what the whale means. The contention here is that Ahab oversteps the limits of understanding in his determination to offer a reading of something about which he has no special information. This allegation has two clear results: it disparages interpretation, or discredits intention-attributing activity as the conduct of the proud and tyrranous; and it suggests that interpretation is something that a man may choose not to indulge in—that there is some other more respectful thing he could do with the objects that make up his world.

When Ahab insists that interpreting the whale is not only feasible but inevitable (something about which politeness has nothing to do), he shows his determination to prove such circumspection false. His resistance is a defense of reading in general, and in particular of reading the incomprehensible other—the being on whose *unquestioned uninterpretability* the respect for its authority hangs. In case a defense of reading sounds unwarranted, note the unpopularity of Ahab's conviction that he can read the white whale—a feat most commonly ranked as a kind of terrible trespass or infringement. But then the insights of old mariners are rarely solicited; these are individuals who speak without being spoken to, who are often considered blasphemous, vulgar, reckless, and ill-advised. Unable to locate decorum's line, they blunder across it. Perhaps, though, crossing the line is not a hazard of the profession but its very purpose.

In the eighteenth and nineteenth centuries crossing the Line, or crossing over the equator, was a sailor's most meaningful act. On a globe by then frequently encircled, the equator was modernity's final border, the last known marker of difference in a blurred world. While only greenhorns could be tricked into thinking the Line could be seen—through tampered-with telescopes—the experience of crossing over was not to be trivialized, as it provided the clearest measure of a sailor's experience, his most prized possession. Experience was the route to knowledge, and knowledge was a sailor's dearest commodity because it couldn't be bought or bargained for—couldn't be stolen or eaten or borrowed against or lost. Having crossed the Line was a sailor's most durable badge of recognition. Having been where others had not, seen more, gone beyond, was what separated able seamen. Here a sailor's authority rested not on commissions or appointments but on experience, and at times like crossing the Line, these distinctions were aired. In *Mr. Bligh's Bad Language*, Pacific anthropologist Greg Dening points to the example of John Gore, who had "been twice round the world with Byron and Wallis" and so "made a novice out of Captain Cook in his first voyage of the *Endeavor*. Cook was made to know that as yet his world was small."

Those who went over the Line often carved the transgression onto their skins—the first tattoos in the Northern Hemisphere were signs advertising a sailor's passage into the South Pacific—but equally significant, if less obvious, were the equatorial theatrics, the dunking and charades, cruel tricks and costumed play that sailors staged as ships crossed over the equator. The ceremonies usually began with a visit by Neptune—rigged out with ropy beard, dolphin skin, crown and trident and deck swab as wig—and his consorts, outrageously jeweled and sticky after careful application of galley fat, bird shit, resin, tar and feathers, grease, and whatever else could be turned cosmetic. Neptune and his court then presided over a kind of trial for those guilty of infringing on Neptune's world, of crossing the Line, or going too far.

The elaborate preparations were the responsibility of those who had already been over the equator, and who eagerly engaged in the mock trials of the virginal—trials, Greg Dening reports, "full of insults, humiliations, injustices, erotic oaths, and compromising choices." Probably the most important part of the ceremony involved ducking. Men were run to the yard by their mates, where they would be strapped to the ducking stool and lowered into the sea—especially horrifying because most sailors in the eighteenth and nineteenth centuries could not swim. A man's capacity to endure the ducking (two times was middling, eleven remarkable) was testament to his bravery and proof of his worldliness. It was, too, a fairly obvious play on being out of one's depth, of being upside down and ass-end up and entirely, terrifyingly at the mercy of your mates (who had been through it themselves and so had little mercy)—of having thrust in your face the absurd, slippery-erotic fact of your trespass into worlds of unguessable depths. It was important that novices understand the seriousness of the act they were about to commit, the irreversibility of its initiations. It was necessary that those who had seen beyond, who had gone too far, were acknowledged for their experience and courage. And it was crucial to mark the occasion, to make a line of it, to put it into words and song.

Thinking to enter and participate in new and strange worlds is risky business—which is one reason why ceremonies of crossing the Line were meant to be terrifying. Without experience, one is bound to feel as if there are rules for understanding to which one does not have access. Experience frees individuals from the impossible task of learning the rules and allows them to negotiate from inside the system in which people act appropriately to each other. It might be said that someone who is inexperienced does not act falsely so much as fail to know how to act appropriately. Trying to function *outside* a network of understanding is like telling a joke to someone who doesn't share your sense of humor. In a letter to Norman Malcolm, Wittgenstein comments that when people do not have the same sense of humor, it feels as if they do not know how to act. In these cases, people do not react properly to each other: "It's as though," Wittgenstein says, "there were a custom amongst certain people for one person to throw another a ball which he is supposed to catch and throw back; but some people, instead of throwing it back, put it in their pocket."

Who has not felt this lump in their pants and wondered at all the quizzical looks? Experience is slippery, strange, unpredictable—knowing how to play the game is never easy. But contracting for any voyage of significance means forgoing the possibility of turning back when threatened with invisible lines, or invisible alliances. Ceremonies like crossing the Line respect the puzzlement that introduction to the new will occasion, but they endorse the crossing nevertheless. These transgressive acts show disinclination to accept the decree that there are parts of the world one will never be able to know, or come to know how, on occasion, to respond. Crossing the Line refuses any strategy of conservation that, in order to preserve the truth, shaves down the negotiable world to regulation size. This bad-mannered unwillingness to bargain away the possibility of knowing is not, however, in the service of the empire or the business of expanding one's territory of control. Crossing the line, or going too far, is potentially an alternative to the more common occurrence of not going far enough, or too easily proclaiming something incomprehensible, inexplicably alien.

The idea that knowledge is relative or preserved in its own indigenous realm (which means that respect for it demands the guarantee of its incomprehensibility) is an easy notion to have in the modern climate but was even easier for a life spent at sea. The constant change in environment invited sailors to reexamine what they knew about the stars, sex, marriage, food, shelter, violence. Such a world offered up a very different experience of the life surrounding the ship, called into question the certainties sailors had come with. Even being a member of a tight shipping community discouraged all hope of confidence. The unpredictability of a sailor's life underscored the arbitrary relationship of a seaman to his institution. The infrastructure of sailoring entailed the necessity of making instant decisions, each of which was subject to interpretation by a superior. Interpretation, to a man before the mast, often invited inappropriate conclusion, and being inappropriate meant being punished. Although the punishment itself was fairly reliable—flogging, casually and clothed or bare-backed and spread-eagled for more serious offenses—the rationale behind the punishment varied greatly. About one-third of all seamen were flogged for "insolence and disorderliness." What counted as disorder or insolence was again usually determined, at sea, by a particular man in a particular circumstance.

To a man shipping before the mast, haphazard fortune appeared to play an extraordinary role in life at sea. Like the weather, aimless fate seemed to infect such important things as a captain's mood (that Cook suffered from intestinal difficulty on his third voyage is a rumored catalyst of his short-temperedness on that trip, potentially contributing to his death in Hawaii), health (suffering from the mystery of "venereals" brought discomfort without much relief, even though a sailor was charged for the visits to a doctor who had no cure), trade (exchanges with natives seemed, to sailors' unschooled eyes, to fluctuate inexplicably between easy hedonism and ready injury), and discipline (on exploratory journeys in the Pacific, Irishmen and Welshmen were twice as likely to be flogged as Englishmen or Scots). At sea, as Dening says, the ordinary right to negotiate what gestures, events, and words meant was often lost.

A mariner is necessarily the most skeptical of all creatures. Thus a mariner's conviction that he knows what something means is an intrepid rejection not of the world's arbitrary quality but of its arbitrariness for *him*. His conviction suggests a kind of reading or engagement, a willingness to venture something concrete about that which has (arbitrarily) come his way. Ahab's determination to recognize his whale, for instance, to know what it means, indicates that while he may not be a good reader of signs, he is a willing reader of signs. To the skeptic's shrug of "who can say?" Ahab's bloody response is *I can.* That this is a poor response, that it somehow misses the point, may be the key to that specific thing the captain of the *Pequod* would like to address. That *something* is missing is the human condition (like an ability to correctly decipher all the signs) but that the proper response to this lack is not despair. The proper response is expectation.

Why one forges ahead has everything to do with attunement to the system in which one is implicated. An object is seen not from a distance but from an experience of neighborliness, from a position of involvement and implication. The object is never viewed impartially—a "complete" view of it is unavailable, as one is always in the picture. Significantly, though, the object is obscured not because the fact of the world blocks one's view of it but because oneself blocks the view: thus the object is never *obscure*—it is always clear to the individual, who need not see all of it to know what it is. To relocate the impediment inside the subject is to change the game. One does not find, unsatisfyingly, that one must come at a thing from a position external to it. From the outside, the world (knowledge, the word) is dead. Rather, one comes to it from the inside of lived experience, from what Wittgenstein will come to call a "form of life."

Negotiation from inside puts a face on things, which makes it possible to talk back or come up with an answer that feels somehow pertinent. As Ahab cries to the spirit fire, whom he "once did worship" but now, burned, knows that "thy right worship is defiance," the only way to keep going is through response: "I own thy speechless, placeless power; but to the last gasp of my earthquake life will dispute its unconditional, unintegral mastery in me. In the midst of the personified impersonal, a personality stands here."

If God is faceless, man is featured. If God is all-seeing, man's vision is narrow, selfish, limited. If God is speechless because he has all of the words, then man has only some of them, a paltry few, but he will use them, even if he has to repeat himself. At the lightning and leap of the flames, Ahab admonishes God: "I own thy speechless, placeless power; said I not so? Nor was it wrung from me; nor do I now drop these links. Thou canst blind; but I can then grope."

The mark of his humanity is his response. That he attempts to talk back to God is a feature of his limitations, he knows, but these limitations are what make him a man. He does not know everything, but only some things: "Oh, oh! Yet blindfold, yet I will talk to thee. Light though thou be, thou leapest out of darkness; but I am darkness leaping out of light, leaping out of thee!"

Obscurity is his medium, but it is exactly this confinement that will free him. That only part of a thing can be seen by him, that something is missing, that he cannot see from all sides—these are the conditions that make human knowing possible. Ahab understands his limitations as *proof* of his ability to read the world; they are what make his world small enough to fit his conceptions of it. That is why he can do to his own miniature world what God can do to his infinite one—comprehend and interpret it: "Here again with haughty agony, I read my sire. Leap! Leap up, and lick the sky! I leap with thee; I burn with thee; would fain be welded with thee; defyingly I worship thee!"

Though Ahab sounds extraordinary, the words he uses are only the old available ones. Part of the romantic notion of bringing the world back to life entails that this can be done with the materials at hand. Blubber, iron, bird shit, deck swabs, nouns, verbs, articles of war. In his earthquake life, Ahab materializes at the scene of the disaster, and it is easy to think him its cause. But as he provides a model of response, of responsiveness, it seems fair to assume there was a question posed to which he attempted a reply.

The most portable form of this question, and so the most sailor friendly, initiates Emerson's accounting of American self-reliance: "Where do we find ourselves?" The longer form of this question is, presumably, Where do we find ourselves in relation to our world? How do we begin the process of looking, and if finding ourselves entails looking for ourselves, does it follow that we must always be both lost and found? By illustrating how to be both lost and found, Ahab volunteers an answer to the most difficult of questions. To follow his lead makes sense because one finds his response appropriate—not his *choice* of response but his choosing to respond. That he comes up with a rejoinder to what many would consider a hypothetical question (posed by a silent universe, so that to speak involves shouting like a child at an uncompromising sky) means he refutes the overcautious presumption that there are some places, some ideas, that are off-limits. *Thou canst blind; but I can then grope.* That in a mariner's world nothing is off-limits does not mean the same thing as everything is within grasp. It simply suggests that the game is personal; from where I stand, all avenues are open. This is so because they are *mine,* shaped and limited by my own peculiarities.

Viewed from this angle, each of us, through ordinary means, can have an everyday intimacy with existence—an intimacy that, as Stanley Cavell suggests, belies or combats a disconnection to the world or a supposed immunity from the demands of the world. To participate in what is called living, we must admit that we share Ahab's blindness and insight. Man is not divinely impartial, open to all possibilities and set on none, but involved, implicated. Pretending to be equitable gods in earthly territory is like posturing in borrowed clothes. Nor does it approximate what is asked of man in the form of worship; man is not asked to like God, or be like him, but is asked to concede, as Ahab does, the *difference* between man and God, a measure of dissension or disagreement that affords the best means of knowing him.

Over such matters *Moby Dick* offers instruction, which strangely makes it a story not about how to go away but about how to come home. What constitutes the feeling of being at home is a sense of comprehension, that one's environment is seen and understood, or that without recourse to any additional interpretive tools one is able to say what things mean. This activity can only be executed from inside lived experience. What gives Ahab the expectation that he knows what things mean is his attunement to the system in which he is implicated—which suggests it is no coincidence that Ahab looks for his whale not just anywhere but somewhere specific.

The *Pequod* is headed in a certain direction, and it is not down. Though in former years Moby Dick had been spotted in the Indian Ocean or Volcano Bay on the Japanese coast, "these seemed only his casual stopping-places and ocean-inns, so to speak, not his places of prolonged abode." If Ahab was to set a course with the best hope of encountering the white whale, if he was to transform whatever wayside prospects were his into a time and place where "all possibilities would become probabilities, and, as Ahab fondly thought, every possibility the next thing to a certainty," then his course was set: "That particular time and place were conjured in the one technical phrase—the Season-on-the-Line." Lingering in these waters, like the sun, was Moby Dick. There "most of the deadly encounters with the white whale had taken place; there the waves were storied with his deeds"; there, where the world's wintry girth was belted round the middle, in this warm trench of the equatorial Pacific, was the whale sure to be found.

But there also in the equatorial Pacific "was that tragic spot where the monomaniac old man had found the awful motive to his vengeance." This sentence is peculiar. It describes the situation in which Ahab found the thing that initiated his future vengeful action. The supposition is that the "thing" is Moby Dick, or more expansively, the encounter with Moby Dick that left Ahab scarred and legless. But technically what Ahab found was not the awful whale but the awful *motive*, which suggests that what he discovered in the Pacific was not the whale or even the skirmish but "that tragic spot." A "spot," as the Season-on-the-Line, which was less a point than a latitude and attitude, already "tragic," before any chance meeting between man and fish—almost as if it was not the whale who caused Ahab grief, but the Line itself. Strange.

But then the Pacific is a strange place, if you're not from there. There is nothing so strange in a strange land, it is said, as the stranger who visits it. But what of the locals? Who *does* inhabit the peculiar place of the Pacific? This deep, spreading sea full of savages? If it is unclear what makes a savage a savage, Ishmael appears to have the answer: savages play life's game, he says, according to chance. In "The Mat-Maker," Ishmael is the attendant of Queequeg, and together they work the loom. In his dreamy state, Ishmael imagines they work upon the "Loom of Time," where the fixed threads of the warp appear to Ishmael as the solid bands of necessity, his own woven thread his particular willed destiny, and the haphazard, sliding instrument of the Maori harpooner the "easy, indifferent" movement of chance. "Idly looking off upon the water," Queequeg "carelessly and unthinkingly drove home every yarn." Ishmael's description of what makes up savagery has something of a child's well-intentioned boast; it is a free, lordly state, one he stakes a claim in: "Your true whale-hunter is as much a savage as an Iroquois. I myself am a savage, owning no allegiance but to the King of the Cannibals; and ready at any moment to rebel against him." The savage's attitude, Ishmael contends, is one of easy surrender to fate, his future open to unplanned possibility.

Here the savage finds a home in as large a sea as the Pacific because he is disconnected and suffers no damning loyalties. But according to this vision whether the savage is admonished for his cannibalcy, applauded for his nobility, or accommodated as part of his colonizer's violent entry, the value of his savagery lies in the unfathomable enigmas of his person. In the first two cases, someone else thinks to speak for him; in the last, no one thinks himself capable of speaking of him, or to him, and so all interpretations of his position are viewed as implausible. Here the guarantee of the savage's authenticity is that he cannot be known, or heard—silence being the only true measure of his purity.

This tourists' picture of locals in the Pacific legislates against their ability to respond, or be responded to. Whose story is this?

According to Ishmael, after Queequeg's miraculous recovery from near death and with a "wild whimsiness," he empties out his coffin and strives, "in his rude way," to copy the tattooing that decorates his body. These designs, it seems, had been the work of an island seer, whose "hieroglyphic marks" contained a "mystical treatise" on attaining truth. But the prophet is now dead and gone, the work unreadable to Queequeg himself, "though his own live heart beat against them," and so the mysteries are "destined in the end to molder away with the living parchment whereon they were inscribed, and so be unsolved to the last." If this be savage, it is the savage brought to you by *The Last of the Mohicans*—quiet, ancient, unsupportable, Hawkeye's repeated antimiscegenational missive the opposite of Christ's in that he swears to "bear no cross." According to this narrative, the best way to respect the savage is to guarantee him his silence. Not unlovable, he is nonetheless an enigma—to himself and his attendants. Ishmael guesses that "this thought it must have been which suggested to Ahab that wild exclamation of his, when one morning turning away from surveying poor Queequeg—'Oh, devilish tantalization of the gods!'"

But in his pursuit of the whale, Ahab supplies a different interpretation of savagery, one that drowns out this terrifying obscurantism in the way that loud, near voices make faraway ones inaudible. His version is one that is more familiar to writers and anthropologists who have spent time in the Pacific and found it not so mysterious a place. Instead of importing grand and coherent generalizations about Oceania, these explorations have generated masses of various and regional information. Here extraordinary attentiveness to detail and small particulars, what ethnographers call "thick description," inch toward exploring the nature of an area known more for its spaces than its places. The leading matter of such investigation must consist of the accumulation of small moments, each more and more familiarly to be enlarged on, until the shape of the thing comes increasingly into view.

How does Ahab gather information? "Had you followed Captain Ahab down into his cabin," Ishmael says, you would have seen him unroll his wrinkled sea charts, spread them on the table before him, "intently study the various lines and shadings" that there met his eye, and "with slow but steady pencil trace additional courses over spaces that were blank." Not only on a particular occasion would one find Ahab at such work, but "almost every night." And almost every night "some pencil marks were effaced, and others were substituted." Ahab does not just study his charts, but he makes them up as he goes along. This is the first defining moment of his savagery and illustrates what he has learned from his time in the Pacific. It undermines Ishmael's (New England) definition that what makes a savage is his strange allegiance to accident and impulse. What reveals Ahab's savagery is his willingness to incorporate new information into his plan of action—and it is his plan, projected onto his very countenance, that reveals him as a savage:

> While thus employed, the heavy pewter lamp suspended in chains over his head, continually rocked with the motion of the ship, and for ever threw shifting gleams and shadows of lines upon his wrinkled brow, till it almost seemed that while he himself was marking out lines and courses on the wrinkled charts, some invisible pencil was also tracing lines and courses upon the deeply marked chart of his forehead.

Ahab is tattooed by the lines and patterns he draws, an inky system he hopes will mark Moby Dick. Here man and whale share the same fate, located as they must be in the crosshatch of these encircling lines. If Moby Dick is somewhere in the ocean, so is Ahab. He is implicated in the map. Nicholas Thomas, writing about the Pacific, insists that its history cannot be understood in terms of class and category but can only be known through "moments of cultural entanglement." When Ahab scales down his charts from the global to the regional, when he finds himself embedded in its particulars, when he adjusts his perspective to incorporate the most current information and in this manner abandons orthodoxy for something less obedient, he is acting like a local.

There are more than twenty thousand islands in the South Pacific. Almost all of the inhabitable ones were inhabited long before Europe made its somewhat accidental discovery of the Pacific and the Pacific made its discovery of Europe. These dots of green sprinkled atop the world's largest ocean were populated by a people who came to them in oceangoing canoes. Even well-provisioned canoes needed a specific destination to survive the open ocean. The feats of navigation needed to perform these acts of exploration and settlement are extraordinary. And savages are known for lives marked by chance?

Ignoring Ishmael's bumpkin conclusions, Queequeg gives his own testimony of savagery. After catching a fever in the hold and showing all signs of a rapid demise, Queequeg suddenly gets well again, much to the astonishment of the crew:

> When some expressed their delighted surprise, he, in substance, said, that the cause of his sudden convalescence was this;—at a critical moment, he had just recalled a little duty ashore, which he was leaving undone; and therefore had changed his mind about dying: he would not die yet, he averred. They asked him, then, whether to live or die was a matter of his own sovereign will and pleasure. He answered, certainly. In a word, it was Queequeg's conceit, that if a man made up his mind to live, mere sickness could not kill him: nothing but a whale, or a gale, or some violent, ungovernable, unintelligent destroyer of that sort.

Queequeg's response, "in a word," is "certainly." And certainty, as Wittgenstein will come to say, is a matter of induction: "The certainty that I shall be able to go on after I have had this experience—seen the formula, for instance,—is simply based on induction." What this means is that I am certain I should be able to continue a series of acts because I feel as if I know all I need to know to take the next step. Like knowing how to go on counting if given the series 2, 4, 6, 8. There are no grounds for this certainty besides pointing to its successes, but as Wittgenstein says, "What could justify the certainty better than success?" Is our confidence justified? According to Queequeg and in the words of Wittgenstein, yes: "What people accept as justification—is shewn by how they think and live."

This is savage talk, which is why the Austrian philosopher must be read as closely as the Maori one when he suggests that "when we do philosophy we are like savages, primitive people, who hear the expressions of civilized men, put a false interpretation on them, and then draw the queerest conclusions from it."

Such comments are often met with distaste, but Wittgenstein is careful, laborious, in his charting. His pencilled corrections are precise: "'But I don't mean that what I do now (in grasping a sense) determines the future *causally* and as a matter of experience, but that in a *queer* way, the use itself is in some sense present." The "falseness" of savages is not to get things wrong, in other words, but to refuse ostensive definition; what something means is not fixed independently from how it is encountered.

This is not Ishmael's early picture of the accidental meetings he thinks define the Pacific. Ishmael's model entails a physical adjustment on the part of the savage in order to accommodate the new. But the real action of savages is to adjust the new in order to accommodate their culture. In this vein, Stephen Greenblatt has made the important distinction between "empathy," which implies a certain modified aspect of the subject, and "improvisation," which suggests the subject adapts not herself but her world: "I shall call that mode *improvisation*," he has said, "by which I mean the ability both to capitalize on the unforeseen and to transform given materials into one's own scenario." The law of improvisation is shaped according to circumstance. The law of the savage is not chance but, surprisingly, convention. In a savage land, things are what you make of them.

(If further testament is needed that haphazardness is not what rules the Pacific, one cannot escape the story of the *Essex,* the fishing industry's most horrible "accident." This vessel was stove in and sunk by a whale, a creature "sufficiently powerful, knowing and judiciously malicious" to use "direct aforethought" to destroy that which was ostensibly out to destroy him. In the textual note, Melville quotes Owen Chase, who had been chief mate on the *Essex,* as saying of the whale: "Every fact seemed to warrant me in concluding that it was anything but chance which directed his operations." Also that it was neither the "dark ocean," nor "dreadful tempest," nor "hidden rocks" that brought terror to the shipwrecked sailor, but only the "horrid aspect and revenge of the whale" that engrossed his thoughts. If you think this denizen of the Pacific gets out of *your* way, the narrator of *Moby Dick* hints, think again: "I tell you, the sperm whale will stand no nonsense.")

The only mystery of the Pacific is its reminder that if you see it, you're in it. What gives Queequeg his authority is his certainty, and what gives him certainty is his feeling of familiarity with his environment, that he is capable of making sense of that which surrounds him. This is not because he sees his world perfectly clearly in an objective sense but because he sees it perfectly clearly in a personal sense. A striving for universal objectivity has no central place in his Maori narrative. He gets his power, his authority, from his connectedness to, his grasp of, the central issues that animate his world.

This connectedness is called, in the Pacific, *mana*. It has been found a difficult term to describe, if only because, like an ocean, it seems to start in the middle and move out in all directions at once. Pat Hohepa, professor of Maori studies, begins an account by calling *mana* a "nonvisible changing measure" that can be inherited as well as acquired. It can be removed by others, or absorbed, or gained through activity, though it cannot be self-imposed if one has lost it. *Mana* is less like a quality than a system that recognizes what a quality is. It indicates the act of being a legitimate part of things, of knowing what to do next. Having *mana* suggests a kind of responsiveness to one's world; it dictates an answering reply, the natural next step. People or events that lack *mana* are not trustworthy: as Pacific anthropologist Marshall Sahlins says, one of the axioms of Polynesian history is that "an action for want of *mana* is a lie." This means not that such an action is deceptive but that it doesn't exist simply because it is outside circulation. It lacks breath. It is not fitting to conclude people without *mana* don't have the right to speak so much as understand they have nothing to say that will have an effect on their audience. It's as if, in the public square, a speaker who lacks *mana* talks in a foreign language.

But in admitting there are instances of cultural incomprehension, one must notice how rare they are in comparison to the countless moments of cultural entanglement—the oceans of shared adventure that swamp the globe. This is because the occurrence of unlike people knowing what one another means does not depend on the impossible luck of having concurring definitions but depends on the individuals' attunement or involvement in the system in which they find themselves. To grasp what someone else means, it is necessary to share, to some extent, their contexts—and sometimes we can't. But the significant point is that individuals need not share the *same* experience to understand each other—only that the one must possess *some* experience onto which the response of the other may fasten, causing the mechanisms of the body and mind to revolve. The most exciting thing about *Moby Dick* is that it describes in detail and with affection this other story, the critical exploit of intimacy without the fantasy of perfect union. In this queer love story, intention and reception do not need to fit perfectly into complementary shapes, but find employment for each other through the habit of application.

Only when I think like a bumpkin do I think I need to be *like* someone to know them, or that it is necessary to follow another person's inner processes to understand him. Here the picture I have in my head is that I somehow need to trace or reproduce these strange experiences. I feel forced to plumb the depths of another's intention—and they are too wide and deep! It feels as if the underwater apparatus I need to interpret their meaning is unavailable, which makes it necessary to resort to guesswork, or to fall to interpreting their hieroglyphic marks. I begin to think of their actions as mystical treatises whose every translator is dead. Where is my Rosetta stone? To regain composure (and protect their private interests), I learn to say I cannot understand them.

But I am forgetting that what is "internal" in this way is not undercover. What is internal is not hidden from me. There is no special key to its mysteries because its meaning is not secret—knowing what something means depends only on my familiarity with the culture that gives it meaning. This idea is encapsulated in one of Wittgenstein's most stunning dictums: "If a lion could talk, we could not understand him." It is not the lion's vocabulary that is missing to us, but his world, the commonality of experience required for all comprehension. It is impossible to understand an alien existence, even if a translating language were made available—but it *is* possible for different people to understand each other as long as the individuals in question share the same criteria for judgment. Because criteria are not private but made from the stuff of public life, the sharing of criteria depends not on perspective but on employment; here *use* of the thing makes gross and unnecessary its *translation*. Criteria are not opinions or rules but the material of experience, the thick, public, imponderable, informative matter that supports a local's feeling of knowing what to do next.

To grant Ahab's native ability to know what to do next (about Moby Dick, for instance) is not to leave him standing outside his society in some excited state of self-regard but to posit in him an intimate involvement in the master fictions through which his society lives. Aha. Ahab. What Ahab offers is a descriptive anthropology, or a broad method of understanding that draws on the full store of everyday human claims, on environmental features that intrude on human subjects, and on the acknowledged events and encounters of those subjects, and seeks, in response to its subjects' affections or habits, to distribute a kind of intelligibility across the features of reality. Thus the "meaning" of the whale is not a property of the whale so much as a way for the people who involve themselves with the whale to come to terms with it. The whale would survive without these terms, but the people wouldn't.

What's more, the words we choose for our descriptions are not timeless but used by certain people at particular moments. Our words adapt, in culturally significant ways, to every occasion. But they do *need* an occasion; words don't mean anything unless they are grouped round a common object. Without this object conversation collapses, expression falls in upon itself, and this is true for the speaker in a crowd or all alone. What people need in order to connect is not a common language (in which different people share the same definitions) but a common object (on which different people may focus their attention). By thrusting his whale into the limelight, Ahab creates a situation in which it is impossible to forget this essential human activity, of gathering around an object for the purpose of saying meaningful things to each other.

Moby Dick is that thing around which Ahab hopes to gather his community and thus make sense of his world. Accordingly the most interesting element of that turnaround chapter "The Quarterdeck," in which Ahab unleashes his vision and binds his crew to the demands of his own appetite, is how willing they all are to go along with it. Ahab assembles the entire company, who mill around apprehensively in the face of their commander's strange, strained expectancy. But suddenly they contract and grow animated; they make fast to a single, fortified voice in response to his cry:

"What do you do when you see a whale, men?"
"Sing out for him!" was the impulsive rejoinder from a score of clubbed voices.
"Good!" cried Ahab, with a wild approval in his tones; observing the hearty animation into which his unexpected question had magnetically thrown them.

It is a brilliant opening to his catechism. If there is anything that binds this assorted, *isolato* collection of men, it is this response to the convolutions of sun and canvas, the one sure thing in a wet, duplicitous world. What do you do when you see a whale? Sing out for him.

"And what do you do next, men?"
"Lower away, and after him!"
"And what tune is it ye pull to, men?"
"A dead whale or a stove boat!"

These are not questions in search of thoughtful answers but an appeal for response already shaped by circumstance. The exchange is not a seduction by Ahab of his crew, or proof of his art, though it is testimony to Ahab's organizing principle. He asks them what they know already. He taps into the only sure thing that animates them and in doing so joins his authority to the authority of the whaling community. This is important; he does not lure them away from their purpose—he confirms it.

Before he tells them of Moby Dick and so perhaps animates hunters' instinct or vengeful accord, before he offers them the gold doubloon or promises financial gain, before he persuades them to take a blood oath, before he muddles their minds with the "honeyed-tongue" of poetry—before there is any Ahab-inspired reason for the joining of this crew and this strange quest, they are aroused and receptive: "More and more strangely and fiercely glad and approving, grew the countenance of the old men at every shout; while the mariners began to gaze curiously at each other, as if marveling how it was that they themselves became so excited at such seemingly purposeless questions." If Ahab has power over these men, it is because they share, at some level, his motivations. Before they drink on the promise (Death to Moby Dick!), Ahab searchingly eyes his crew, looking for discontents: "But those wild eyes met his, as the bloodshot eyes of prairie wolves meet the eye of their leader, ere he rushes on at their head in the trail of the bison."

Only Starbuck, for whom cash and compromise have more magnetic pull than any fishy philosophy, must be persuaded by Ahab. And though he will always prove a sticking point, a suited salesman at a Harley convention, Starbuck eventually operates under basically the same impetus that leads the crew into such easy compliance; Ahab's seemingly inordinate demand is more ordinary than it appears—it's just what is done anyway. "And what is it?" says Ahab of this hunt for the white whale and Starbuck's participation: "Reckon it. 'Tis but to help strike a fin; no wondrous feat for Starbuck. What is it more?" This small, deferential shrug to make a conservative man complicit has been most often read as a line no better than "Haven't I seen you around here before?" but there is truth to it nonetheless. For whatever it is that drives Ahab to kill this particular whale drives, in lesser degrees, these other whale killers. Even Ahab is surprised by the resonance of their response. He says to himself, when alone, "'Twas not so hard a task. I thought to find one stubborn, at the least; but my one cogged circle fits into all their various wheels, and they revolve."

It is a beautiful moment for Ahab, this compliance that disproves his alienation from the living centers of society. One assumes, from the view the shore affords us, that the farther out to sea the *Pequod* travels, the closer it comes to chaos—that the crew are slipping away, that to come home to some kind of order (represented, in seaman's tales, by a young wife and a warm bed) will bring them nearer to the reason why they go out in the first place. Ballocks. Whatever order orders Ahab is found in the wake of the whale, not ripped apart by it. And the captain says it plainly, when Starbuck accuses him of poor logic: "'Vengeance on a dumb brute!' cried Starbuck, 'that simply smote thee from blindest instinct! Madness! To be enraged with a dumb thing, Captain Ahab, seems blasphemous!'" As if taking a child in hand, gently, gently, Ahab remonstrates with his first mate for being so literal. It's not the whale that's the thing, Ahab says. His scheme is not the stupid one of retribution. Ahab's purpose is to reveal the ways in which man is connected to things less like a curious spectator than like a confederate and collaborator. He fingers himself as a chargeable accomplice in the rather violent act of interpretation:

> All visible objects, man, are but as pasteboard masks. But in each event—in the living act, the undoubted deed—there, some unknown but still reasoning thing puts forth the mouldings of its features from behind the unreasoning mask. If man will strike, strike through the mask!

And Moby Dick is a coconspirator, in league with Ahab in this fierce rendering of a whale. Moby Dick is not a villain but an opportunity: "He tasks me; he heaps me; I see in him outrageous strength, with an inscrutable malice sinewing it. That inscrutable thing is chiefly what I hate; and be the white whale agent, or be the white whale principal, I will wreak that hate upon him." The "inscrutable thing" is what Ahab hates and what he directs his animus against. It is Starbuck who first calls his captain's pursuit "vengeance." Why believe him? Starbuck is the doltish, imperfect marriage of false twinkle and ready money. A sugar high. A bad investment. Better to take Ahab at his word and share his imperfect quest. Without Ahab, Moby Dick is no familied member of the Pacific, no hoary uncle to the Grand Armada; he is, sans Ahab, a cruiser, an opaque mangler with no affiliations. (Quiet your Greenpeace hearts.) In pursuing him, Ahab does not throw meaning, with caution, to the wind. He tries to impress it onto that white surface, like ink on a page.

(I should say here, in case it is not obvious, that I am pointing to Ahab not as a literal example of how one should act but as a literary example of thought's action, of the activity of knowing what things are. Ahab is the stuff of which thought is made. I mean to incite not whale killing, in other words, but whale reading.) What Ahab brings to life, in his preoccupation with Moby Dick, is the philosophical understanding of what it is to see something as something. His certainty about what he is doing is an illustration of the way in which perception works. Like the captain of the *Pequod*, perception does not hesitate, and it does not misrepresent. It knows what it is looking for, it knows where to look, and it is never wrong. However, it does, thankfully, take shape under a facilitating and neighborly influence, what Wittgenstein calls "forms of life," and what is sometimes called culture. Because perception is indivisible from its context and use, it cannot help but act in the interests of its hosting community, the apparatus that breathes life into its truths. (How Ahab can ever be said to act in the interests of his community will be a point taken up more fully in this book's conclusion—but what must be understood for the present is that Ahab's authority is based on his embeddedness in a public narrative.)

Ahab's involvement with the whale makes clear by what means the creature will be captured—by a language sufficiently complex and elastic enough to speak with authority about things unspeakably slippery, submerged, and colorless. This language depends on having a system of support that makes it impossible to *not* know what a word means—it relies on culture. Culture is not what makes it feasible to translate the words of another into words of one's own—there is never any key strong or flexible enough to crack the secret code of another. Culture is whatever one has to comprehend in order to behave appropriately to other members of society. Culture is what enables individuals to know, without turning to translation, what one another means.

The reward of the search for Moby Dick is not the death of the desired object, the whale, but the capture of it, the flash of sense that makes a sighting possible: the insight, the trick—the key to understanding not just this fishy thing but any secret intelligence. What Ahab establishes is not the meaning of a thing, not the meaning of a word, not the meaning of a whale, but *readability*. His is an ingenious plan that is never not itself; an alphabet; a performance that will generate infinite rerecordings. What Ahab offers is the sense of connection, of patterns being discerned, when everyone else has dully subsided into resigned confusion.

{ 6 }
A LEAKY BOAT

We are aware of ourselves, for we are aware of others,
and in the same way as we know others; and this is
as it is because in relation to ourselves we are in
the same [position] as others are to us.
— *Lev Vygotsky,* Thought and Language

IN THE LANGUAGE OF THE FISHERY, a whale needs no
secret code. The whale itself is the Rosetta: feed it the barest
theme and it takes on a certain, unmistakable shape. But say I
shout from the riggings of the *Pequod,* "Whale!" How does my
sentence manage to represent? How does my "Whale!" cross the
distances between speakers and remain recognizable? How do
you understand this whale? How do you understand *"this"*? As
Wittgenstein says in *Philosophical Investigations,* "The whole idea
of understanding smells fishy here." Meaning is slick and unfettered. As long as there is no connection between words and
things, it feels as if the wind must pick up my words and inad-
vertently deposit them elsewhere. I feel I am forever shouting
from the rigging.

Out in the world, language is what Iris Murdoch calls "a
colossal infinitely various creative ferment." Adrift in the sea of
this unsolid substance and deprived of customary support, it is
easy for those who must rely on language to lose their faith in
it. Caught without rock or hard place, they begin to flounder in
a morass of anxiety and skepticism. But what the whaling industry teaches is fortitude—or rather, it has little tolerance for the

strange comforts of total depravity. It finds instead that it is not necessary to give up the game at the first signs of adversity— only to carefully trace what is wrong with our understanding.

The first problem is the belief that what speakers do with words is read them for direction, as if in order to make sense of a word I must follow its counsel about what kind of thing it is. According to this scenario the word "whale" leads me to search my mind for the right definition of it, which sends me looking for an appropriate image, which encourages me to say that I know what this word means. But how do different speakers come to use the same definitions? And what if there is no image? Lots of words don't have what we call images, like "this," for instance, or "for," or "instance." There is even a problem with the ones that do, like the word "whale." As the sometime narrator of *Moby Dick,* Ishmael points out that very few people have an accurate image of the creature. This is because those with the mind and leisure to draw the thing, he says, "never had the benefit of a whaling voyage (such men seldom have)" to fortify their visions. Thus they are likely to make ridiculous child's play of the task, producing something gormless and flat: "Frederick Cuvier's Sperm Whale," says Ishmael, "is not a Sperm Whale, but a squash." But those who do get close enough to the creature rarely have the drawing-room time to complete the record, as "the only mode in which you can derive even a tolerable idea of his living contour, is by going a whaling yourself; but by so doing, you run no small risk of being eternally stove and sunk by him."

The problem of representing the whale cannot be solved logically, by way of bringing that uncapturable thing, the leviathan, into a safe space from which to view him. If long dead, the whale's skeletal frame cannot speak to its living form: "For it is one of the more curious things about this Leviathan, that his skeleton gives very little idea of his general shape." Unlike a human's "articulated bones," the mere skeleton of the whale "bears the same relation to the fully invested and padded animal as the insect does to the chrysalis that so roundingly envelopes it." Nor can the whale be fully witnessed in man's proper medium, air: "Though elephants have stood for their full-lengths, the living Leviathan has never yet fairly floated himself for his portrait. The living whale, in his full majesty and significance, is only to be seen in unfathomable waters; and afloat the vast bulk of him is out of sight, like a launched line-of-battle ship." The point here is that to know the whale, one must know him alive, and at sea. The whale is not a whale unless in the context of an ocean. It cannot be divorced from its world and thought to be understood: "Only in the heart of quickest perils; only when within the eddyings of his angry flukes; only on the profound unbounded sea, can the fully invested whale be truly and livingly found out."

Like a whale, a word will not sit still for its portrait. Words are not, by themselves, in the business of representation. Words don't point to things. So what is it about words that makes their meaning clear? Disconcertingly I find that when I use the word "whale" in the old way, as if it pointed to something, the thing it points to is not there—or if it is there, it has probably expired. There is nothing in the word that helps me to the *live* whale. Nothing shows me the way. Nothing about the word tells me what to do with it. It lies there like a dead thing, beached. The more careful I am with it, the more painstakingly I examine it, the less sure I am that it has anything to tell me. A skeptic can now feel justified in saying that words lack the fortifying gestures that make their meaning apparent. But imagine: a parcel of whalers strolling along the shore come across the huge wasted carcass of a spermaceti. Who would be the first to cry "Whale!"?

When, that is, does a word *ever* entail instruction concerning what to do with it? The skeptic creates a puzzle for himself by scrutinizing the abyss between a word and the object it hopes to capture. Convinced by the disconnection between word and thing—objects being too often abstracted, episodic, dead, or wanting documentation—the skeptic assures himself that he confronts an uncrossable distance. But then, he wonders, how does anyone know what he is talking about? If words aren't connected to things, how do they make their meanings manifest? His problem is that although he knows a word is not a label, he still has the sense that a word does what a label does—provide direction, or point to something, as if the word itself must tell him what to do. The skeptic, having spent too much time alone, thinks that for the word to be meaningful, it must speak to him. For the skeptic, the word "whale" must say clearly, "I am a whale!" He waits, slack-jawed, for a response from the carcass. When it does not come, he thinks language has failed him.

By reviving that which these skeptical deliberations have laid waste, it is possible to restore language to its original health. Instead of working its way from sense data forward and so eventually ending in a skeptical position, the "whale" hunting language philosopher begins by demanding an investigation of *how* one recognizes a word. She learns her lesson from the industry, which insists that one comes to the meaning of "whale" *without* direction; whaling demands being influenced by whales in such a way that at the moment of encounter the meaning of the thing is clear. A whaler does not begin with the object, the whale, and then look for connections from it to herself. The *whale* does not tell her what to do with it. At sea, a whaler cannot afford to wait for the whale to provide directions but must rush up to it, never stopping to think about how he knows what it is.

Whaling is whale employment, which means that it is not the whale that is ultimately brought into reference but the interpretants of this thing *whale* that determine its representation. (Thus we should quit saying that the *whale* symbolizes such and such, when it is really man's symbolic capacity we are talking about. Otherwise the slovenliness of our language, as George Orwell said, will make it easier for us to have foolish thoughts.) Because reference is created by the nature of response, the meaning of the whale derives from the process of generating some cognitive action, some interpretive reading. But even if we get clear about the meaning of the creature, how does the *word* "whale" get its meaning?

According to the industry, in quite ordinary ways. As Wittgenstein says, the fact that I *use* this alien and alienating thing, language, implicates it in the ordinary and commonly available working world (the world that works). To differentiate this used, useful version of language from the stilted, ineffectual picture we have of it, Wittgenstein coined the phrase "language-game." The difference he means to establish is the difference between a two-dimensional thing, a flat representation, and a practice with depth and volume, that which invites and depends on reception. The term "language-game" is meant to "bring into prominence the fact that the *speaking* of language is part of an activity, or of a form of life."

I should like to say that a living word doesn't speak to me so much as involve me in its achievements. It takes hold of me; it lays siege to my mind. I do not feel instructed or informed by it so much as annexed to it. At any rate, a good "whale" hunter is exasperated by any philosophy of language that establishes an individual's grasp of a word as equivalent to reading it for direction. Directions only work if you sort of know where you are—if you know what someone means by "hang a left" or "look for the fork in the road." This describes a funny way of getting one's bearings, saying that only someone who knows how to use them could significantly ask for directions—but we cannot forget that this is how directions work. And once again the lesson (that explanation *trails* comprehension) is a trademark of the fishery.

Whaling is an activity in which one is expected to find whales without really looking for them, capture them without really seeing them, and proceed with all the confidence of one born to such a role. It is an enterprise made possible by the particular kind of advance that seems to begin in the middle, or from the inside. What Wittgenstein means by "language-game" is similar: there is no point at which a language user comes to the meaning of a word fresh, outside the system that has made it available. He famously considers this case:

> I am explaining chess to someone; and I begin by pointing to a chessman and saying: "This is the king; it can move like this." . . . In this case we shall say: the words "This is the king" . . . are a definition only if the learner already "knows what a piece in a game is." That is, if he has already played other games, or has watched other people playing "and understood"—*and similar things*. Further, only under these conditions will he be able to ask relevantly in the course of learning the game: "What do you call this?"—that is, this piece in a game.

This kind of explanation works only because the ground of its meaning is already prepared. This is so "not because the person to whom we give the explanation already knows the rules, but because in another sense he is already master of a game."

What does it mean to be the master of a language game? What does Wittgenstein indicate by the term "mastery" here? *Moby Dick,* I am suggesting, offers explicit instruction in what Wittgenstein means by mastery—especially in how it is a concept designed to be inclusive, or used in mixed company. For Wittgenstein, mastery of a language is what one needs to use it. Mastery of a language keeps us from having to learn it, or repair it, or find it in pieces. "Of course you have *mastery* of this language," says Wittgenstein, speaking to anyone who uses words meaningfully. But how does this mastery happen?

How mastery happens for a whaler is illustrative. The measure appears to invoke the difference between Ishmael on his first whaling voyage and Captain Ahab on his last. Captain Peleg, interviewing Ishmael for a place on board the *Pequod,* is horrified by the greenhorn's lack of whaling knowledge. Ahab the weathered seaman, he seems to suggest, is the model of mastery against which Ishmael's innocence must be measured:

> "Dost know nothing at all about whaling, I dare say—eh?"
>
> "Nothing, Sir; but I have no doubt I shall soon learn. I've been several voyages in the merchant service, and I think that—"
>
> "Marchant service be damned. Talk not that lingo to me. . . . Marchant service indeed! I suppose now ye feel considerable proud of having served in those marchant ships. But flukes! Man, what makes thee want to go a whaling, eh?—it looks a little suspicious, don't it, eh?—Hast not been a pirate, hast thou?—Didst not rob thy last Captain, didst thou? . . . what takes thee a-whaling? I want to know before I think of shipping ye."
>
> "Well, sir, I want to see what whaling is. I want to see the world."
>
> "Want to see what whaling is, eh? Have ye clapped eye on Captain Ahab?"

According to Peleg, a man who is not a whaler has little chance of becoming one, as he speaks a different language. But in Peleg's dismissal of a sailor's experience lies a clue to what mastery really means.

Peleg suspects Ishmael of piracy or criminality because he can't imagine what a merchant sailor would want on board a whaler. Ishmael, protesting his innocence, thinks of the old seaman "as an insulated Quakerish Nantucketer . . . full of his insular prejudices, and rather distrustful of all aliens, unless they hailed from Cape Cod or the Vineyard." Ishmael, under Peleg's scrutiny, feels himself born outside the circle. Not a Quaker, and not a Nantucketer, a whaler he will never be. He understands the Quaker captain to be saying that what experience Ishmael does have as a merchant sailor brings him no closer to his goal. "Marchant service be damned," Peleg says. "Talk not that lingo to me."

But Ishmael only half guesses the precision of Peleg's decree. While it is true that there is no way to become a Nantucketer except by birth, and no way to become a whaler except by whaling, this model does not leave Ishmael forever outside his chosen profession. What it does is eliminate the possibility of training. Peleg's warnings amount to the suggestion that no measure of familiarity with other kinds of sailoring is going to prepare Ishmael for the whaling industry. There is no stepping-stone into whaling. It is a difference not of degree, between Ishmael and Ahab, but of kind. Either you are a whaler, or you aren't.

The humor behind Peleg's innuendos suggest a whaler's sense that such a proposition should come as a relief. Mastery, according to the whaling industry, is not something one acquires in stages. Ability, of course, is recognized through a pecking order, and increasing levels of skill are rewarded through profit and prestige. But if a sailor undertakes a whaling voyage, then he is by definition a whaler (unless he is a criminal and a liar). Before he ships, Ishmael is not a whaler; afterward he is one. Whether he is bad at it or not does not affect his mastery of this thing. In the whaling industry, according to this interview, mastery does not mean the ability to do one's job faultlessly; it means the ability to do one's job.

Herein lies the explanation for why whaling must be said to be a grammatical industry. Though I think that I learn how to speak by acquiring grammar, in fact, in order for me to speak, a grammar must first be intuited. This seems like an impossible paradox, as if I must learn all of the words to begin to learn about any one word. Agreeing to this contradiction is like saying that to understand ostensive definition, I must already be master of a language—because when I talk about language, I must already be speaking it. When Peleg asks Ishmael why he wants to go whaling, Ishmael's response is "Well, sir, I want to see what whaling is. I want to see the world." Peleg teaches Ishmael a difficult grammatical lesson. What words he needs, he knows. What world he hopes to see, he's already seen:

> "Now then," says Peleg, "thou not only wantest to go a-whaling, to find out by experience what whaling is, but ye also want to go in order to see the world? Was that not what ye said? I thought so. Well then, just step forward there, and take a peep over the weather bow, and then back to me and tell me what ye see there."
>
> . . . Going forward and glancing over the weather bow, I perceived that the ship swinging to her anchor with the flood-tide, was now obliquely pointing towards the open ocean. The prospect was unlimited, but exceedingly monotonous and forbidding; not the slightest variety could I see. . . .
>
> "Well, what dost thou think then of seeing the world? Do ye wish to go round Cape Horn to see any more of it, eh? Can't you see the world from where you stand?"
>
> I was a little staggered, but go a-whaling I must, and I would; and the Pequod was as good a ship as any.

Running the length of his dismissal of the bumpkin is Peleg's suggestion, bordering on the obvious, that Ishmael will become a whaler by becoming one. It is the warning that there is no such thing as preparatory training for such a task—but also the assurance that one is already master of all the tools necessary to do the job. There is, in other words, no impediment to a view of the world that moving your arse is going to fix. Being a better whaler will not make you a better viewer—as the world, like the whale, cannot be approached in a gradual manner, as if by degrees. Like a squirrel chasing itself around a tree, no matter how far or fast it moves forward, it still has the whole circumference of the tree before it. No matter how far over the horizon Ishmael sails, his view of the world remains the same—not because he cannot help but keep outside it, a visitor to its edges, but because he maintains his original position, the one he has already mastered, of being inside the world.

When I allow myself to think that words offer instruction, I tend to envision the stretch between me and meaning as a distance I need to negotiate. I think my problems in explaining how words connect to their meanings stem from an inability to command a clear view of the use of words, to see them as if from all angles. I convince myself that if I could just see the picture (of a word) more clearly, get in a better position, just move these few last obstacles from the way, then, *then!* As this attempt proves too exhausting, I fall away from the world, thinking the space of it too big.

But the beauty of ordinary language philosophy is in the simple lesson that language does not refer outside itself, because in "giving explanations I already have to use language full-blown." As Wittgenstein says, "When I think in language, there aren't 'meanings' going through my mind in addition to the verbal expressions: the language is itself the vehicle of thought." In order to speak at all I must speak the language of every day. "Is this language somehow too coarse and material for what we want to say?" Wittgenstein asks. "*Then how is another one to be constructed?—*And how strange that we should be able to do anything at all with the one we have!" That we can do anything with the language we have suggests that it is adequate to our uses. This means that language does not delude us but is essentially honest; if I think it somehow fails my purpose, it is I who am the liar and the pirate. There is nothing wrong with the vehicle. Upon finding what it means to "see the world" from a whaling ship, Ishmael admits that "the Pequod was as good a ship as any."

Grammatical influence means that words themselves don't need to guide us or tell us what to do. When we use words, we do not wait for instruction. Skeptics are right to think that there is no way to take direction from a word, but wrong to think that this inability suggests one cannot use language meaningfully. This is because knowing what words mean has almost nothing to do with taking direction. When we think about coming up to a word, or knowing what it means, we must act like whalers: "When we mean something, it's like going up to someone, it's not having a dead picture (of any kind)" says Wittgenstein. "We go up to the thing we mean." There is no hanging back. When one means something, "one is rushing ahead and so cannot observe oneself rushing ahead. Indeed not." "Yes," Wittgenstein says for the third time, "meaning something is like going up to someone."

How could using language possibly be the product of such mindless propulsion? How could it be otherwise? If we waited for words to tell us what to do—instead of rushing ahead, going up to words, incriminating and damning ourselves in the chase—how could we use words at all? I can give you directions, "Meet me over there" or "Look at this!" but "there" is not a place, and "this" is not a thing. To be able to follow such advice, you must first know where you are going. You must already be launched on the pursuit of a word before you can be said to know what to do with it. A word does not point to sense but is itself inscribed in a system of support that makes not knowing its meaning impracticable. Wittgenstein calls this ocean of imponderable evidence "grammar," and says that it is impossible to ever know a word unless one is immersed in its world. The suggestion is that we do not approach words like strangers but recognize them like friends. Or less benevolently, we do not take cautious steps toward them but hurl the whole of ourselves at their nearest recognizable parts. Words, if one is to be in relationship with them, if they are to be used, must be gone up to, rushed upon. There can be no hanging back.

Native speakers, in other words, do not employ the qualities associated with *following* when employing the meaning of a word. Following a word depends on thinking there is some distance (which one may track) between a word and its meaning. But language philosophers insist there is no difference, no space in which to negotiate, between words and their meanings. Thinking it is possible to start looking for the meanings of words suggests thinking about words' meanings as something separate from the words themselves. As if one could get off (on) a word without admitting the meaningful influence of its expression. How is this dismount accomplished? It recalls Augustine's sense that words have certain meanings and speakers learn them. And there is something odd about saying that words *have* meanings, as if the meanings accompany them like handbags. Meaning is not an accessory. A word and its meaning are made of the same material.

I use words according to certain rules, and these rules, Wittgenstein says, are not followed but obeyed: "When I obey a rule, I do not choose. I obey the rule *blindly*." Using words is less like following their meanings than obeying their meanings; it's as if the words assail me, as if I fall prey to them. There is no time for them to tell me what to do once I am in their clutches. When we use words, Wittgenstein says, we do not follow directives or wait for them to instruct us: "One does not feel that one has always got to wait upon the nod (the whisper) of the rule. On the contrary, we are not on tenterhooks about what it will tell us next, but it always tells us the same, and we do what it tells us."

Words don't tell us what to do with them; they tell us what to do with ourselves. For a large number of cases in which we employ the word *meaning*, Wittgenstein says, "It can be defined thus: the meaning of a word is its use in the language." The word simply does not breathe outside the domain of its use, as the whale does not live outside its watery world.

So how do I come to terms with this state of affairs? The whale is inseparable from his context—to know him, something like the whole of the ocean must be factored into the equation. But oceans—Atlantic, Indian, Pacific—differ; does the whale change as he swims from one to the next? Must I rename him at each new feeding ground? A poet would say yes, but a poet does not depend on hunting the whale for his supper. A whaler must be able to name the thing he has killed (and so brought permanently out of the context of an ocean). Wittgenstein has concluded that it must be so—otherwise language ceases to hold up meaning: "What the names in language signify must be indestructible; for it must be possible to describe the state of affairs in which everything destructible is destroyed. And this description will contain words; and what corresponds to those words cannot then be destroyed, for otherwise the words would have no meaning." Or colloquially, "I must not saw off the branch on which I am sitting."

It is not necessary to abandon a name even while its meaning changes situationally. This can be expressed: I use the name "W" without a *fixed* meaning. Does this mean that my concept of "W" is a blurred one? And is, as Wittgenstein asks, "a blurred concept a concept at all?" Melville's answer appears in the affirmative, if his chapter entitled "Monstrous Pictures of Whales" is any guide. His narrator's warning (those who can't draw, do; those who can draw, die) is embedded in a work undertaking the very thing he complains of; "I have had to do with whales with these visible hands; I am in earnest; and I will try." He promises "nothing complete" but states at the outset that his system of classifying or depicting whales "would not be here, and at once, perfected. . . . God keep me from ever completing anything. This whole book is but a draught—nay, but the draught of a draught." Melville promises blurred concepts. In the way of cetology, what he offers is inexact, his romantic object something one can get very close to, but not something one can see *all* of.

At sea, in the thick of things, a view of a whale is only ever a partial view. But the fact that at best man can see only part of this thing in its habitat, and that he risks a considerable amount in the attempt, does not mean that the thing—the whale—cannot be seen. Unless by "seen" I mean seen in its entirety, an all-or-nothing approach that does an injustice to the ordinary meaning of the term. Consider the statement "I saw my mother this morning." Did I really see all of her? The soles of her feet? Would it make sense to say that I did *not* see my mother this morning—that I *met* with her but did not *see* her? What would she say about the accuracy of this account, especially if afterward she went missing and I was called on to give a description of her to the police? When I use the word "see," I do not intend it to mean "see all of," but only "see enough to make sense of," which amounts to the same thing as "see what is interesting to me."

Isn't this depiction inexact? And why shouldn't I call it inexact? As Wittgenstein says, though, I should be clear about what "inexact" means: "For it does not mean 'unusable.'" Early in *Philosophical Investigations* Wittgenstein poses the possibility that it may not be an advantage to replace an indistinct picture with a sharp one. "Isn't the indistinct one often exactly what we need?" he asks. His explanation of why a blurred picture may be preferable to a distinct one echoes Melville's suggestion that the most accurate portrait of the leviathan is a blurry one. Precise images of the whale are necessarily false, as they must be taken from a strange, Godly distance—far enough to be seen in entirety but near enough to be seen with absolute precision. Whalers, Melville keeps reminding his readers, have the best pictures of all men, and their pictures are obscure—at their best, the furred, disproportionate visions of something dangerously close. As his crew enters the churned, charmed circle of the whale, Stubb makes explicit their necessary approach: "'Pull up—pull up! . . . Pull up!—close to!' and the boat ranged along the fish's flank." Because of whalers' regular vacillation between tremendous distance and staggering proximity to the object of their attentions, whales are creatures impossible to capture, as Ishmael says, with "any very considerable degree of exactness."

What ordinary language philosophy does is put blurred concepts to use. Noting Frege's declaration that an area with vague boundaries cannot be called an area at all, and understanding that this implies we can have no use for it, Wittgenstein wonders if it is true that a suggestion like "Stand roughly there," indicated by an open gesture, really isn't helpful. Presumably one could follow such direction and be subject to reproach—"No, not there, *there!*" But this is in fact how the game is played. When I give examples of what I mean to a bystander, my intention is that they are to be taken in a certain way; I do not, however, as Wittgenstein argues, "mean by this that he is supposed to see in those examples that common thing which I—for some reason—was unable to express; but that he is now to *employ* those examples in a particular way."

The difference between interpreting an example and employing one is the difference between searching for the essence of a thing and understanding its use. If I want you to know exactly what I mean, to understand the essence of what I am saying, then the logic I use is one that pertains to what Wittgenstein calls a "peculiar depth." This kind of logical explanation "seeks to see to the bottom of things and is not meant to concern itself whether what actually happens is this or that." Those who seek this essence do not look for something that lies "open to view" but look instead for something "that lies *beneath* the surface." Such an inquiry hopes to "eliminate misunderstandings by making our expressions more exact"; but in its attempt to measure a thing's perfect value, this logic sinks further and further beneath the surface of actual events until it comes to rest, like sunken treasure, on a sandy floor. This kind of search "may look as if we were moving towards a particular state, a state of complete exactness; and as if this were the real goal of our investigation," but its result remains out of living reach and at the bottom of the sea.

The search for a whale, or whales, might seem at first like a perfect illustration of looking for the essence of a thing, of using logic of a "peculiar depth." Whales are creatures famous for lying beneath the surface. That they do not lie open to view would seem to exclude them from any consideration of what Wittgenstein, at least, would call philosophy. But *Moby Dick* is an instructor's manual, and one of its purposes is to correct such misunderstandings concerning the whale fishery.

Take, for example, the particular instance of the white whale. A landlubber might imagine the task of finding him to be an extraordinary one, as the possibilities of his whereabouts encompass the whole of the ocean. Because this thing dives, seeking it out takes place not only on an impossible surface but at an impossible depth. What's more, "finding" it, to a landsman, means finding all of it, knowing it in a state of complete exactness. He thinks that he must somehow see beneath the surface, a proposition that leaves him gasping for breath. Confidently, he suggests that such a search is foolhardy, nay, unfeasible— outside the bounds of human ability. "See how high the seas of language run here!" Wittgenstein warns.

But a whaler knows better than to assume that to find a whale the whole of the ocean must be at one's disposal. The narrator of *Moby Dick* explains that "to any one not fully acquainted with the ways of the leviathans, it might seem an absurdly hopeless task thus to seek out one solitary creature in the unhooped oceans of this planet." But a whaler like Ahab "knew the sets of all tides and currents; and thereby calculating the driftings of the sperm whale's food; and, also, calling to mind the regular, ascertained seasons for hunting him in particular latitudes; could arrive at reasonable surmises, almost approaching to certainties, concerning the timeliest day to be upon this or that ground in search of his prey."

Perhaps the search is not so foolish, after all, narrowed as it is by reason and instinct to a thin river of possibility. Hypothetically

Ahab's whale could be anywhere in the ocean, but chances are, he isn't: "When making a passage from one feeding-ground to another, the sperm whales, guided by some infallible instinct . . . mostly swim in *veins*, as they are called; continuing their way along a given ocean-line with such undeviating exactitude, that no ship ever sailed her course, by any chart, with one tithe of such marvelous precision." Though the veins in which these whales are said to swim generally embrace some few miles in width, this distance "never exceeds the visual sweep from the whale-ship's mast-heads, when circumspectly gliding along this magic zone. The sum is, that at particular seasons within that breadth and along that path, migrating whales may with great confidence be looked for."

In *Moby Dick* whalers don't look for whales in the manner that landlubbers think they do. The view from the masthead discloses "whales" only by seamen's terms: what whalers look for, and what they find, are spouts of water shot into the air (a whale is distinguished from other expiring creatures by the number of seconds between blasts) or circling seabirds (eating the sea macaroni off a broad back) or giant squid (a favorite prey). Whalers do not look for some fully invested caricature of the whale, floating above the surface or swimming in its crystalline waters. They find whales by employing the signs of their whereabouts. Employing signs does not entail reading them for meaning (squid does not *mean* "whale") but involves using them to get one's bearings, so that when the thing that is being pursued appears, one can look right at it, without hesitancy, without looking away to see what it is.

Thus when a whaler goes about looking for a whale, he doesn't seek the essence of a creature at a peculiar depth but employs whatever signs he needs to go on, so that he can go on in a certain way. Whalers are immune to the misconceptions of philosophers who believe in their genius for revealing what something *is*. Whalers don't care about depth; most whalers don't even know how to swim. But they can say they know a whale because they employ its meaning in specific ways. *Whaling* is whale employment. (The nature of Ahab's investigation was never whale representation, but whale employment—of which he was always master.) Employment of an example forgoes the urge to see all of a thing, to get at its essence, and instead wants to put to use something that is already in plain view.

But why would this activity lend itself to philosophy? As Wittgenstein says, "The aspects of things that are most important for us are hidden because of their simplicity and familiarity. (One is unable to notice something—because it is always before one's eyes.)" Wittgenstein gives the name "philosophy" to the difficult work of investigating that which is right in front of us: "Something that we know when no one asks us, but no longer know when we are supposed to give an account of it, is something that we need to remind ourselves of. (And it is obviously something of which for some reason it is difficult to remind oneself.)" Wittgenstein firmly declares that the "aspects of things" with which we must concern ourselves are not *hidden* but hard to see because they are easy to see.

What gives the whaling industry philosophical significance is its refusal to find meaningful only that which reaches beneath event. Whalers know that when they say "whale" there is no meaning of the word going through their minds—the "whale" itself is the vehicle of thought. The suggestion is that words don't *have* meanings but are meaningful; or as Ahab understands it, whales do not *lead* to concepts but are concepts. And concepts, Wittgenstein says, "lead us to make investigations; are the expressions of our interest, and direct our interest." Here it is not the word "whale" that has any depth, but knowledge of the value concept "whale" that is deep. A whaler does not switch on to the given impersonal network "whale" but comes to it with a history, a cultural narrative. This is funny, but true: whalers bring what might be called depth to whales, which they find on the surface.

Regarding a whale—or having a use for it, recognizing it, seeing it as something and not another thing—demands that a subject draw upon the full range of his or her experiences and distribute, across the features of that whale, a kind of intelligibility. We should say that in the *living* event, the "unknown but still reasoning thing" (that which is not oneself but with whom one has dealings) "puts forth the mouldings of its features from behind the unreasoning mask" (presents itself for a reading, which we are obliged to give it). Attributing intentionality to objects amounts to what we call *interpreting* them. As there is no alternative to reading things in this way, we should speak of interpretation not as a kind of bad habit, not to be fully trusted, but as real knowledge.

What whaling does is put into service that which is in plain view—but not at all in the way a behaviorist might. Whaling transports the notion of certainty from the outside to the inside; it shows how one *can* have "knowledge" of "appearances." The world says that Ahab can't know Moby Dick's true significance because the whale's meaning is secreted, as it were, inside its form. But a whale hunter will never tolerate such nonsense, especially when the philosophical work that needs doing is less like exposing the world's objects than remembering their connections to us. Whaling is the business, after all, not of wrenching off but of *striking through*.

That is, "meaning" according to the industry, is a public matter—and this is so not simply in regards to Moby Dick. Ahab's actions suggest that not only does he know what the whale means, but he also knows what "whale" means—not only when he says it but when anybody else does too. Readers of *Moby Dick* are called upon to say that they, too, know what Ahab means when he says "Whale." Now the argument for finding the proposition "I cannot know what Ahab means" more untrustworthy than the proposition "I know what he means" is generated by the assumption that the thing that disproves my ability to know what someone else (Ahab) means is my own ability to know what *I* mean. But "knowing what I mean" entails translating my words to myself while I am using them—which, by all accounts, is not what I do. If the skeptics were right, why does our language find them out? Why then, Wittgenstein wonders, is it grammatically correct to say "'I know what you are thinking,' and wrong to say 'I know what I am thinking.' (A whole cloud of philosophy condensed into a drop of grammar)"? To think that what someone else knows is hidden from me, and therefore unemployable, is a false conclusion. Saying I cannot know what someone else means is like saying a whaler cannot find a whale in the ocean because he will not be able to see all of him. A thing never becomes meaningful because it is seen in its entirety, but because enough of it is made use of by one who comprehends such proceedings.

Ahab's whale is not imagined, nor is it strictly discovered, but is found, by him, which suggests that it has an existence separate from his but also that it depends for its coherence on something extra he supplies, some conception of his own, which makes sense of things. Just as the whale cannot be prized away from Ahab's manner of conceiving it, so is it impossible for Ahab to escape his own conceptual scheme, which suggests that man and whale impress themselves on each other in ways meaningful to each. Thus Ahab's business with Moby Dick jettisons the prevailing suspicion that semantically it is impossible to proceed with confidence, or say what something means, because one's subjectivity gets in the way. Man's perception of an object and the object percieved are not separate, nor are they they same. A whale, like any other thing, is the consolidation of foreign and domestic affairs.

In *Moby Dick* Melville attempts to document this awesome occurrence (the making/knowing of a thing, like Ahab's white whale, which is both an object and an idea) in the only mortal way possible. His strategy is to rely on the exhaustive accretion of minutiae, on the one hand, and amplification and embellishment on the other. The one tactic provides the foundation for fact, and Melville gathers examples like tiny mollusks and sea macaroni into a shelf substantial enough, after a while, to become a reef, something that holds back the tide. As Ishmael testifies: "Since I have undertaken to manhandle this Leviathan, it behooves me to approve myself omnisciently exhaustive in the enterprise; not overlooking the minutest seminal germs of his blood, and spinning him out to the uttermost coils of his bowels." The other, more boastful and romantic, is what gives the concept its scope. The awkwardness of this attempt makes appropriate actions that in other circumstances may be deemed what Melville calls "unwarrantably grandiloquent," but "when Leviathan is the text, the case is altered":

Fain am I to stagger to this enterprise under the weightiest words of the dictionary. . . . How, then, with me, writing of this Leviathan? Unconsciously my chirography expands into placard capitals. Give me a condor's quill! Give me Vesuvius' crater for an inkstand! Friends, hold my arms! For the mere act of penning my thoughts of this

Leviathan, they weary me, and make me faint with their outreaching comprehensiveness of sweep, as if to include the whole circle of the sciences, and all the generations of whales, and men, and mastodons, past, present, and to come, with all the revolving panoramas of empire on earth, and throughout the whole universe, not excluding its suburbs.

The task is inclusive and without reserve, and one must be, like the ocean, relentless. Because contemplation of any one thing—a whale—is only possible through association with the whole thing, the world. This is what it means to be lost. Where do we find ourselves?

When I stand among these mighty Leviathan skeletons. . . . I am, by a flood, borne back into that wondrous period, ere time itself can be said to have begun, for time began with man. Here Saturn's gray chaos rolls over me, and I obtain dim, shuddering glimpses into those Polar eternities, when wedged bastions of ice pressed hard upon what are now the Tropics . . . Then the whole world was the whale's; and, king of creation, he left his wake along the present lines of the Andes and the Himmalehs.

One finds, like *Moby Dick*'s narrator, that examination of the whale pries loose the rim and brings us to the very brink of conventional perimeters: "Ahab's harpoon had shed blood older than the Pharaohs'. Methuselah seems a schoolboy. I look round to shake hands with Shem. I am horror-struck at this antemosaic, unsourced existence of the unspeakable terrors of the whale, which, having been before all time, must needs exist after all human ages are over." That a whale's genealogy is as wide as the world is why the narrator of *Moby Dick* solemnly warns his audience that it is in this "Afric Temple of the Whale I leave you, reader, and if you be a Nantucketer, and a whaleman, you will silently worship there."

How can one ever hope to navigate under such conditions? Ever the sullen guide, Ahab is as usual most right when acting most wrongly. In the chapter "The Quadrant," Ahab addresses his tool, and finds it does not speak back to him: "Thou sea-mark! thou high and mighty Pilot! thou tellest me truly where I *am*—but canst thou cast the least hint where I *shall* be? Or canst thou tell me where some other thing besides me is this moment living? Where is Moby Dick?" In his search for the whale, Ahab has cottoned on to the truth of navigation. It is not enough to know a single point, if that point signals no relation. Seeing the cabalistic contrivance of his quadrant for what it is—a lonely man's single pinprick, linking him not to the world but to an imagined heaven—Ahab heaps curses upon it: "Foolish toy! babies' plaything of haughty Admirals, and Commodores, and Captains; the world brags of thee, of thy cunning and might; but what after all canst thou do, but tell the poor, pitiful point, where thou thyself happenest to be on this wide planet, and the hand that holds thee; no! not one jot more!"

Here is Ahab's final rejection of his private parts. The eye of the quadrant goes up, as to God, not out, as into the sea: "Curse thee, thou vain toy; and cursed be all things that cast man's eyes aloft to that heaven. . . . Level by nature to this earth's horizon are the glances of man's eyes; not shot from the crown of his head, as if God had meant him to gaze on his firmament." Savvy to the Ancient Mariner's manly mistake, Ahab intuits that when reading for meaning, he must spread outward, not look upward. Net-working is more likely to catch him his whale: "'Curse thee, thou quadrant!' dashing it to the deck, 'no longer will I guide my earthly way by thee; the level ship's compass, and the level dead-reckoning, by log and by line; *these* shall conduct me, and show me my place on the sea. Aye,' lighting from the boat to the deck, 'thus I trample on thee, thou paltry thing that feebly pointest on high; thus I split and destroy thee!'"

Poor Ahab, to be so clever, so staunch, so feminist, and in such feeble company that his revelations are met with revulsion. Notes an unrecalcitrant Ishmael of his captain and his plight, "Here, then, was this gray-headed, ungodly man, chasing with curses a Job's whale round the world. . . . morally enfeebled also, by the incompetence of mere un-aided virtue or right-mindedness in Starbuck, the invulnerable jollity of indifference and recklessness in Stubb, and the pervading mediocrity in Flask." As usual Starbuck also reads his captain badly, regarding Ahab's fiery rejection of his tool with a disapproving eye. Like Ishmael, Starbuck takes Ahab's tendency to turn to the things of this world as turning away from God. (Blast that Starbuck! He tasks me; he heaps me. His inscrutable thing is chiefly what I hate.) But Ahab is simply paying his best allegiance to God—worshiping at the Temple of the Whale—by admitting earthly connection, commensalism, symbiosis. Righteous Starbuck predicts Ahab's ashy incineration but is blind to his captain's integrity:

> "I have sat before the dense coal fire and watched it all aglow, full of its tormented flaming life; and I have seen it wane at last, down, down, to dumbest dust. Old man of oceans! Of all this fiery life of thine, what will at length remain but one little heap of ashes!"
>
> "Aye," cried Stubb, "but sea-coal ashes—mind ye that, Mr. Starbuck—sea-coal, not your common charcoal. Well, well; I heard Ahab mutter, 'Here some one thrusts these cards into these old hands of mine; swears that I must play them, and no others.' And damn me, Ahab, but thou actest right; live in the game, and die in it!"

Starbuck knows enough to call Ahab an "old man of oceans," but it takes Stubb to explain what that means. Ahab knows himself implicated; unlike Starbuck he never forgets for a single moment that he is at sea. Whatever the tools of Ahab's rescue, they will also be the machinery of his imprisonment. There is no way to operate from a position external to the world. Starbuck, under the impression that there is always a safe place to rest and reassess, still thinks like a landlubber. He advises his captain that in a time of danger, they should make for the safety of the shore:

> "The oil in the hold is leaking, sir. We must up Burtons and break out."
>
> "Up Burtons and break out? Now that we are nearing Japan; heave-to here for a week to tinker a parcel of old hoops?"
>
> "Either do that, sir, or waste in one day more oil than we may make good in a year. What we come twenty thousand miles to get is worth saving, sir."
>
> "So it is, so it is; if we get it."

"I was speaking of the oil in the hold, sir."

"And I was not speaking or thinking of that at all. Begone! Let it leak! I'm all aleak myself. Aye! leaks in leaks! not only full of leaky casks, but those leaky casks are in a leaky ship; and that's a far worse plight than the Pequod's, man. Yet I don't stop to plug my leak; for who can find it in the deep-loaded hull; or how hope to plug it, even if found, in this life's howling gale?"

Wittgenstein's best hopes for philosophy, what Ishmael calls "worshiping at the Temple of the Whale," is the dignity of fixing a leaky boat while at sea. What Ahab hopes to find in his pursuit of the whale is the ability to overhaul without the pretense of thinking himself capable of leaving the water. The nobility of his plan should not be underestimated. It is what is meant by staying in the game—never thinking to get out of the water, but remaining in the boat, too.

Intimately involved with the torment of trying to fix a leaky boat while at sea, philosophy that hopes to survive with integrity investigates ways to proceed under such circumstances. What if the answer does not lie in trying to escape the situation—as Pip does, when he leaps from the whaleboat? That way lies madness. Or, as Starbuck suggests, in thinking it possible to find safe ground. Neither suicide nor denial is an escape from meaninglessness, only its dramatization. But suppose, as Wittgenstein says, that the "real discovery is the one that makes me capable of stopping doing philosophy when I want to.—The one that gives philosophy peace, so that it is no longer tormented by questions which bring *itself* into question."

It would be a terrible mistake to understand this last reasonable remark from land as advocacy for a Starbuck-type capitulation, of finding peace by turning home or giving up the chase. What it means to stop doing philosophy, for a whaler or an ordinary language philosopher, does not entail coming to a rest. It amounts to the type of circumstance in which someone knows how to *go on* in a certain way. The peace not of stasis but of headway. To take an unhesitating step there must be some sense that I have guessed the nature of the path correctly—that I could be said to "understand" what is expected of me. What must happen to justify a person saying that in such a case she knows how to go on?

It's a question of influence. Wittgenstein has shown how my saying "Now I understand" does not rely on my having learned all the rules but depends on my employment of the signs that come my way. In *Moby Dick* what is called for is this ability to read the objects of one's commissioning. The first thing its author knows is that one must rely on words, not pictures, for the whale's capture, nor is it possible to take direction from words so much as experience them, participate in their employment. Using language is like being part of a culture, part of the crowd, part of a storm. Which means that the second thing a whale author knows is that because words are his medium, they must touch, like the sea, multiple shores.

Philosophy that echoes the practice of whaling opens up the world by opening the word—by suggesting that the only way to know what a word "means" is to recognize it in its various meanings. Here language is learned not by direction but by implication. Only from the thick of things, from inside relationship to stuff and event, can a study of language, hence philosophy, be compelling. In this case inextricability, which spells out the demise of any distinction between inner and outer, should be a solace. This joins the project of *Philosophical Investigations* to that of *Moby Dick,* the undertaking one of finding *comfort* in the fact that philosophy is like fixing a leaky boat that must be repaired while at sea.

On the occasion of Ishmael's first lowering, this is what happens to his boat: Under the command of Starbuck, the crew is giving chase to three whales when a squall comes upon them. The desperation of their pursuit is matched and heightened by the fury of the sea, so that "with the still rising wind, we rushed along; the boat going with such madness through the water, that the lee oars could scarcely be worked rapidly enough to escape being torn from the row-locks." Though in the midst of the storm, the crew still has a job to do. They continue to pursue the whale, even though the chase augments the danger of their situation:

"That's his hump. *There, there,* give it to him!" whispered Starbuck.

A short rushing sound leaped out of the boat; it was the darted iron of Queequeg. Then all in one welded commotion came an invisible push from astern, while forward the boat seemed striking on a ledge; the sail collapsed and exploded; a gush of scalding vapor shot up near by; something rolled and tumbled like an earthquake beneath us. The whole crew were half suffocated as they were tossed helter-skelter into the white curdling cream of the squall. Squall, whale, and harpoon had all blended together; and the whale, merely grazed by the iron, escaped.

Though completely swamped, the boat was nearly unharmed. Swimming round it we picked up the floating oars, and lashing them across the gunwale, tumbled back to our places. There we sat up to our knees in the sea, the water covering every rib and plank, so that to our downward gazing eyes the suspended craft seemed a coral boat grown up to us from the bottom of the ocean.

They are lost to the ship, lost to the other boats, and their situation seems hopeless. Starbuck lights a lantern and passes it to Queequeg, who holds up "that imbecile candle in the heart of that almighty forlornness." They sit and wait until dawn comes on, when "despairing of ship or boat, we lifted up our eyes. . . . The mist still spread over the sea, the empty lantern lay crushed at the bottom of the boat."

But suddenly "Queequeg started to his feet, hollowing his hand to his ear. We all heard a faint creaking, as of ropes and yards hitherto muffled by the storm. The sound came nearer and nearer; the thick mists were dimly parted by a huge, vague form." It is, of course, the ship—out of sight, but not of hearing. The crew leaps from the boat just in time to avoid being knocked to splinters by the hull of the vessel bearing blindly down on them. Ishmael's early lessons are, first, that looking for something is a less reliable practice than listening for it: the candle Queequeg was given to hold, "the sign and symbol of a man without faith, hopelessly holding up hope in the midst of despair," added nothing to their rescue—its light only illuminated the darkness. What Queequeg recognizes is not the shape of the ship but its sound. And second, the supposed object of rescue carries its own threat; the ship, suddenly upon them, is almost the means of their destruction.

Back on board the *Pequod*, what most surprises Ishmael—a man new to the fishery—is that in the midst of such a dangerous squall anyone would continue to hunt a whale. Because even through the foam and rising waves Starbuck was heard to whisper dangerously, "There is time to kill a fish yet before the squall comes. There's white water again!—close to! Spring!" *Starbuck!* After the calamity, Ishmael turns to Stubb, who is calmly smoking his pipe as if there were never any cause for alarm, and asks him the wisdom of such tactics. To find oneself at sea is one thing; at sea in a storm another; but at sea in a storm and thinking to give chase to a whale?

> "Mr. Stubb," said I, turning to that worthy. . . . "Mr. Stubb, I think I have heard you say that of all whalemen you ever met, our chief mate, Mr. Starbuck, is by far the most careful and prudent. I suppose then, that going plump on a flying whale with your sail set in a foggy squall is the height of a whaleman's discretion?"
>
> "Certain. I've lowered for whales from a leaking ship in a gale off Cape Horn."

Stubb echoes Queequeg's conceit, when asked if he thinks to dictate the hour of his death. Certainly. To be certain means knowing how to move ahead, where to take the next step. But how does an experienced seaman manage the incongruity of how tenuous and perishable a man and his flimsy tools seem in comparison to his improbable purpose—how puny and ridiculous his "prey" makes him appear? If man could somehow see himself from outside of himself, he would certainly appear tiny, transient, unduly susceptible to injury and insult. But from where one stands there is no such picture. In the real world of our participation, the difference between our efforts and our insignificance evaporates. In an existing context there is no authentic conflict between the subjective and the objective, or the inside and outside, only the practical consciousness that arises from what Melville calls the "stubbornness of life."

What happens when I understand something, when I suddenly know how to proceed, is that the circumstances of my condition allow me to say that I know how to go on. This is what ordinary language philosophy teaches: an individual's immersion in the world is what makes it possible—unavoidable—to go on in a certain way. Trained by the relativists to find personal conviction limiting, a modern philosopher might well object, with one of Wittgenstein's imagined interlocutors, "But, if you are *certain,* isn't it that you are shutting your eyes in the face of doubt?" Wittgenstein's reply: "They are shut." Certainty is not a measure of purity, available through an unimpeded vision of an object; it is a sense of expectation, possible *because* I do not see everything, which suggests how I am to go on. Certainty depends not on my ability to see all of something but on my ability to pull up to it—*close to!*—to enter its charmed circle, or its grammar, its sea. Like Stubb and Queequeg, I can, on any particular occasion, be certain because certainty is culled from conventional material, and as such it is bedfellow to prudence.

Knowing the next step does not depend, then, on having one's present conditions perfect, or perfectly explained. Which makes this statement of Wittgenstein's—"Philosophy is like a leaky boat that must be repaired while at sea"—not a warning but a promise. Of course philosophy is a leaky boat that must be repaired while at sea; where else would a boat be found out as leaky? Stubb's version—"I've lowered for whales from a leaking ship in a gale off Cape Horn"—suggests that the least ideal moment to hunt whales is no cause for missed opportunity, since the most ideal moment for hunting whales is unimaginable. What would the most ideal moment be? One always has to start in the middle, from the thick of things. Thinking to better the boat, better the weather, is like thinking it possible to hunt whales from land.

But what of the landlubber's apprehension—that he teeters in an infirm craft over a kind of emptiness? He thinks that to get across this sea, he needs to plumb its unfathomable depths. Worse, he's riding in a leaky contraption, and it appears that he is responsible for fixing it but somehow lacks the tools. This all seems terrifying because he wants to apply what Wittgenstein calls the law of excluded middle. This law says, "It must either look like this, or like that." Either he floats above the fray, or he drowns. Either all the world is contained in his mind, or he loses his mind in trying to explain how the world works.

Another way of explaining the landlubber's problem is to say that he feels trapped between the extremes of realism and idealism—separating matter entirely from his perceptions or reducing matter only to the image he has of it. Extreme care over the decision of what counts as trustworthy seems like an obvious choice to give him back the sense of a solid foundation, but such caution works only by unnecessarily limiting the range of his senses and understanding—depositing him, as it were, on a small spit of land and forbidding him to set foot in the ocean. This carefulness amounts to the suggestion that to postulate objective truths, he must ethereally tenant the viewpoint of an impersonal intelligence. Everywhere the landlubber looks, he sees no other possibility—if he plays sailor and thinks to see the world for himself, he fears he will suffer shipwreck, with nothing but water and his own sinking vessel in sight.

The feeling that there can't be a third possibility, says Wittgenstein, "expresses our inability to turn our eyes away from this picture: a picture which looks as if it must already contain both the problem and its solution, while all the time we *feel* that it is not so." The means of this saving grace is not coming into view over the horizon. It already lies open before us. We think the problem is the sea that lies between us, but the sea that lies between us is the answer!

I am baffled by the puzzle of how to get from *here* to *there;* how I can tell you to go there and hope to find you there—how I can tell anything at all. But I am going about this the wrong way. I am trying to get myself onto dry land, into a dry boat, forgetting that the "gulf between an order and its execution . . . has to be filled by the act of understanding." At sea the contradictions of a leaky boat evaporate, in part because seamen know that to align a feeling of certainty with isolation from the world, and a feeling of skepticism with immersion in the world, is to play the game backwards. Certainty is found in relation. I know a word because I know the world it inhabits. I know a word because it comes swimming into focus. For an order to work, I must understand it as I apprehend it. An ocean touches distant shores; when I put my finger in the water off the Californian coast, I touch the same sea that washes the sands of Japan. Language is like the ocean, which is why Wittgenstein can say that "it is in language that an expectation and its fulfillment make contact." Whenever I speak I am at sea—my words are surrounded. The picture I have in my head of being in a leaky boat seems to show that my circumstances (being at sea) are what stand in the way of any future certainty. When in fact my circumstances (being at sea) are exactly the state that supports my actions. They are what justify my knowing how to go on in a certain way. *Whenever* I speak I'm at sea. Which means I am in no need of rescue.

SWAN SONG

We despise obvious things, but from obvious things
unobvious ones follow.
— *G. W. Leibniz*

I HAVE TRIED TO EXEMPT, from the wrongness of Ahab's
life, any conclusion that he was wrong about his *whale*. But the
truth of his one great insight still leaves the twisted, stinking
hulk of this story intact. If *Moby Dick* is, as I believe it to be, a
story to live by, it is only fair to consider the ethical implications
of Ahab's position, both prior and subsequent to his garroting
by the harpoon's line. Is his death—by his own instrument, in
a swamped boat after witnessing the sure destruction of his
ship, so that before his neck is cut he is "cut off from the last
fond pride of meanest shipwrecked captains," to go down with
the vessel and crew—some kind of retributive justice? Is his
hanging, with no one and nothing to stand under him, fairly
warranted? "Oh lonely death on lonely life!" The question for
moral consideration is, does so *public* a man as Ahab—the last,
gross, concentrated accumulation of nautical accident and infer-
ence, in whose wasted carapace lie the piled centuries of man's
own loves and disappointments—deserve so sequestered and
forlorn an end? Or perhaps the better question, for those who
think his humiliation proper: on what deliberations do these
retaliative judgments lie?

If Ahab's lonely end is indeed the cursed fate of leaders
who make unscrupulous decisions or gamble the lives of their

charges without consideration, then to declare his administration in any way ethical would be to make a mockery of the appointment. The allegation leveled against him, which so clamors for his annihilation, is that he risks not only his own life in the pursuit of his whale but the lives of his unwilling men: "Oh, Ahab. Ahab, lo, thy work," cries Starbuck, in his final hour. So is the first mate, then, finally right, and Ahab's self-indulgence his only legacy? Certainly it is difficult to argue that as a man in charge of a company, Ahab knows what to do with his own best intuition: that it's the day-to-day stuff that lets us know who we are, the thickness of ordinary life that tells us what things mean. (And, given the expansiveness of this measure, the human inclination to furnish this pond of activity with some reasoning force is acceptable—because you really do need a system if you're going to make it work, some administrative purpose.) What Ahab fails to comprehend, though, is that the system comes included with the life—it doesn't need to be sought out except as illustration. Interpreting the world or its objects is not possible because one gets oneself into a special position to do so; interpretation is certain and inescapable because an individual's ordinary station in the world makes it so.

Ahab's failure to know that meaning-making activity is safe, however, is unlike contributing to or ensuring the collapse of his *crew*'s safety—the negligence for which the captain stands accused. Does Ahab's chase after the interpretable object really necessitate a loss of life or freedom or choice for everyone else on board the *Pequod*? According to the popular account, yes. What makes the novel tragic and Ahab the helmsman of this tragedy is his insistence that his crew members' lives are inconsequential next to the momentous business of his pursuit. Or less dramatically, that their investments and attachments are subordinate to his. Poor Ahab, to have so long suffered under this misconception of his undertaking! But before welcoming this lost brother once again into our confidences, it is essential to imagine Ahab less indifferent to his fellows than he seems.

Assuming *Moby Dick* should be classed as a tragedy, what makes it so? As *Moby Dick*'s pro/antagonist, what constitutes Ahab's hamartia is that while he is of all seamen best able to delimit the system of maintenance or supportive grammar that keeps man on his course and tells him what things are, the captain fails to find *himself* properly supported. He thinks of his own form, after his encounter with Moby Dick, as imperfect, half-baked; a razed, limping burlesque; a "poor pegging lubber" left to wobble on a dead stump. Worried that he is unequal to the task at hand—of finding purpose in the world's activity—he abandons the easy satisfaction of knowing what things mean for the discontent of proving (to a nonplussed public) that things are meaningful. Feeling crippled, ill-made, or somehow at a disadvantage leads Ahab to believe he is in need of better tools—augury or sorcery—to succeed.

But Ahab's savvy, his whaler's sense of how the world is held together, should have affected at all levels his process of coming to a conclusion. When Ahab bemoans the loss of his leg or ties his dismasting to his claim on the whale ("Aye . . . It was Moby Dick . . . that brought me to this dead stump I stand on now"), he points to his missing gam as the explanation for the disunity that incites in him such antagonism. Too bad that in philosophy, as Wittgenstein says, "We do not draw conclusions. 'But it must be like this!' is not a philosophical proposition." To think to chart from event to result with a desultory *because* is not what philosophers do. And what makes Ahab a complex character is that he knows better than to simply link his injury with his hostility—why else would he spell out to Starbuck his reading of Moby Dick? Why call him tragic at all? The captain is not suffering under a misconception. Ahab's attempt to strike through incomprehension does not call for an account but gives one, which indicates that his lameness is *not* what puts him at a disadvantage. What lets Ahab down, finally, is not that missing limb, nor even his academic objection to the creature who took it (*he* does not cut off the limb on which he is resting).

So who does swipe from beneath him his native system of support? Perhaps it is those under him who disappoint Ahab, rather than the other way around. According to the stock denunciation of the captain's behavior, Ahab fails his community because he refuses to cut his ties to them when calculating his own risky, probably fatal, obligations. (If it is not clear how Ahab's hunt for the whale is an obligation, not a conceit, then call this for the moment my failure, not the captain's.) It isn't fair, according to Starbuck's perspective, that Ahab's investment in the white whale be extended to his crew—especially when they have not contracted for such an undertaking. Starbuck's response to Ahab's hope that he will also promise to hunt Moby Dick indicates what Starbuck sees as the difference between the obligations of his job and the ordainment of his captain: "I am game for his crooked jaw, and for the jaws of Death, too, Captain Ahab, if it fairly comes in the way of the business we follow; but I came here to hunt whales, not my commander's vengeance." Starbuck resists being made party to Ahab's "indissoluble league," and it is easy to think him right for doing so. As usual, though, it is necessary to look more closely at Starbuck's account of freedom, independence, and fidelity, for here lies some opportunity for catastrophe.

Take the most obvious case on board the *Pequod* in which one man's loyalties determine another man's fate—the disorderly business of cutting-in and attending to a whale. The individual whose actual business it is to cut into the whale (as the creature is strapped half-submerged to the ship's hull) is tied to an individual on the relative safety of the deck, so that if he who is in the most immediate danger sinks to rise no more, "both usage and honor" demand that instead of cutting the line, the unmolested sailor who manages one end of it is dragged down in his fellow's wake. It is a humorously perilous occupation, this knowing of a whale, and demands of its participants a thick confidentiality. Each a one is strung by snapless cord to any other. In such business there is no room for guiltlessness, as another's mistake or misfortune might plunge any bystander to unmerited disaster.

Starbuck wishes these ties cut. As the first mate would have it, an individual at risk may hope for assistance from his associates, but the outer reaches of their accountability to him is sentimental—if they understand his predicament or share his perspective, they might come to his rescue, when convenient, but there is no obligation to do so. (The sentimentalist, it seems, suggests that he loves you because he understands you, an arrangement that Stanley Cavell calls a "metaphysically desperate degree of private bonding." The sober unsentimentalist, unwilling to lose the object of his or her affection simply because of dull incomprehension, does not say, "I love you because I understand you," but "I love you because I *am* you." This last declaration may sound no less metaphysically desperate, but it speaks to the type of connection made possible only by a kind of living investment. The sentimentalist still thinks it possible to find a thing at once distinctly separate from him and entirely available to him; the unsentimentalist finds himself *in* the thing.) At any rate, Starbuck's recommendation is to be only *relatively* available to neighboring influence. He takes care of himself and others by being subject to his community's interests but not contracted to them in any disagreeable manner—when, for instance, these interests become menacing or unruly. Starbuck's efficient solution to the problem of otherness is for an individual to know himself to be so separate and dissimilar from his associates that he may cast off from them when his investments, or theirs, become a liability.

Does Starbuck remember (do we?) that the jeopardy to which a whaler may be hazarded is just as likely to be psychological as environmental? Not only is the man at sea vulnerable to inclement weather, accident, and injury, but he is also exposed to the possibility of not knowing how to go on in a certain way, a habit of despondency that makes more attractive certain retreats from meaninglessness—like resignation, for instance, or self-destruction, the firm foundation of unyielding despair. The first thing man misses as he leaves the shore behind is his confidence. His right to determine what things mean. His interpretive ability. Thus the danger represented by the fishing industry is not just personal, the dangle of one fellow's limbs too close to his snapping nemesis, but sweeping and indiscriminate. It includes the world's coherence and intelligibility—all participation, all ordinary expectancy, all habit of human genius. If every eagerness, every comforting solace, must inevitably be buried beneath the debris of a universe incapable of knowing itself, then there is nothing for it but to collapse in the deepest humiliation. Well, if this light goes out, this light goes out, says Starbuck. If every man can only count, finally, on his own small understanding of the world, then he must take whatever caution necessary to protect his own person; at least, if he succeeds, someone may escape to tell the story.

Here the moral dimension of Ahab's monomania comes swimming into view. To Starbuck's sketch of relative accountability, the only appropriate response is refusal—absolute refusal to partake of such high-priced self-interest. What Ahab's interdependent model offers, to those willing to signal their involvement, is that in the event of some calamity to your person, all hands will be on deck to lend their support. In exchange you must acknowledge that you share the concerns of others—which, by all ordinary accounts, you do. It means admitting there will be no action of which you are a party but to which you are indifferent, or in which your investments are not also entirely sunk. In this public scene there is a kind of rude appropriation, an off-kilter, unpredictable reaching out to the unoffending bystander, who only dully comprehends, too late, the inadequacy of his claim to innocence.

Ahab lives in a web of transactions, and his acumen and his anguish grow out of his transactional life. There is a kind of forced wretchedness to Ahab's activities, of reason being constantly stretched to its limit—but if his neighbors feel the strain of his attentions, is it not right that it be so? And doesn't this connection guarantee support for their own fond perceptions? What Ahab brings to light is the impossibility of cutting ties to the objects of one's interest. That these ties are often fastened at an anchoring end to one's associates is more often than not a saving grace.

Ahab's lesson, more moral than it seems, is that the person with whom you share a history—this is the person who can leave you shipwrecked and drowning. Although this sounds bleak, it is meant as a piece of optimism. It suggests that one is connected to the world and its objects in such a way that when someone goes missing, he will be sorely missed—or that another's misfortune might plunge the seeming innocent into disaster, thus mortally wounding the concept of "free will" and forever changing narratives of escape and survival. If it is true that when an individual is destroyed, so are all who knew him, the safe and dry are forced into a state of dependency, a state destined to afford the strongest possible guarantee to the imperiled. This monkey-rope ensures a measure of response and responsibility that often evades sentimentality.

How, then, do we go about safeguarding each other from our varying interests? As the objects of our investments are sure to be different, what mechanisms do we have for distinguishing the interests of the cabin boy from the interests of the captain? In Ahab's particular case, what is clear is that there is no golden rule that would protect the crew of the *Pequod* while its captain exposes only himself; to say to Ahab that he should never do to others what he wouldn't have done to him is no measure of safety, as there is nothing, it seems, that Ahab wouldn't suffer to secure his desired object. If what is required from him is a kind of moral hesitation, by which he may see that what is right for him or calls to him does not necessarily call to someone else, this inhibition will derive from a source quite different from philosophical universalizing.

What we want from Ahab is consideration of other positions, that perspectives entirely different to his will somehow impinge on his decision making—because to be considered conscientious, a perspective must needs move imaginatively between its own position and that of others. It must ferry back and forth between these familiar and foreign ships, like any captain who wishes to consult with another vessel's commander while at sea. But if one must move in imagination back and forth as often as necessary between one's own and a neighboring position, how is this accomplished with any degree of success? Perhaps a more fitting question for the officers of the *Pequod,* armed and readied as they are for the worst, is the one concerning which conduct will *prohibit* the required transit between oneself and others. Is there a program or course more likely to damn its practitioner to his own private ruin?

Starbuck's hope is to maintain a kind of margin of coolness, or space of autonomy, around the innocent (or only slightly complicit) party. He does so in the attempt to save them—or more likely save himself—from being forced to pursue objects in which he or they have little investment. Indifference, according to this view, is the surest method of preservation. As Starbuck sees it, Ahab is incapable of upholding his duty to others because he has on the whole failed his first obligation to himself—to choose, by his own free will, from among varying investments. According to Starbuck, Ahab's unwillingness to turn away from the whale is what consigns him to hell. But to this proposition the scoundrel Ahab rejoins that he's *in hell,* thus mocking Starbuck's decorous and straitlaced notion of the world's division into neat categories, with borders man may overstep and edges he may fall from. In what universe do such borders and edges exist? Ahab submits that there is something more dreadful than a world in which all creatures swim the same waters, and that is a make-believe world in which nothing can be meant and of which little can be said. Whereas I have in the past primarily treated Starbuck as a kind of archfiend, it would be a disservice to the first mate not to admit that *in the main* we share his expectation and his goal—the observation and protection of difference. While it is true that only from a standpoint of immanence can the world be lived in (the captain and crew are all aboard the same leaking ship; they belong to the same world, which is the only world there is), Ahab and the crew *live* such a world so differently that in effect they also live in different worlds. Just because Ahab and the crew are in a relation of mutual interdependence, it does not follow that they are one with Ahab and that the objects of their interest are the same as his. Had this story been told by anyone else aboard the *Pequod*, it would certainly have had a different direction and device.

So let us be clear: we do not disparage Starbuck's *objective*, but his *method*—and it is Starbuck's method that Ahab turns his attention to destroying, with the packed arsenal of his once-dormant ferocity. The fact that under Starbuck's wretched custody the opposition lost doesn't mean that in the pursuit of the white whale *all opposition* is lost—only that Starbuck proved ineffectual as its superintendent. At the core of Starbuck's policy (where Ahab had hoped to encounter a heart but found instead a machine) are the two principles that shape the first mate's standard of conduct: (1) the best way to extend autonomy to others is by insisting they cannot be known; and (2) the objects of man's interest are created and maintained privately and thus must be privately pursued.

According to Starbuck's view, the surest way for Ahab to emancipate and protect his peers is to promise that he cannot know them or know their minds. This theorem proposes that knowing is private, the furtive and clandestine activity one keeps to oneself. It protects otherness by ensuring it can't be interpreted. Starbuck also insists that whatever Ahab's investments, they should be pursued in private and without the involvement of his crew. His suggestion for Ahab is that all experimentation with the whale—whatever it takes to "capture" it, understand it, use it, read it—must happen in or under careful isolation. (So if Ahab wants to go after Moby Dick, he must do so without the aid of his crew.) According to this view, one's investments are personal and particular, singular perversions that should only be explored, if at all, by oneself.

Of course, to prove that Ahab can't know the minds of his neighbors, Starbuck must depend on the premise that Ahab can know his own mind or know himself like no other. But the intention of this study has been to show how Ahab can only know himself *like* he knows his neighbors—or be said to know himself only in the same neighborly ways in which he knows anyone else. In a radical departure from Starbuck's antiquated cognitive model, the captain's contrivance, more in keeping with actual brain function, blurs distinctions between the manner in which we know others and the manner in which we know ourselves. It makes meaningless the claim that Ahab knows himself in ways different to the ways he knows someone else. What's more, Ahab's refusal to provide a secure but dangerously simplified re-creation of this thing *whale* attests to his sense that to reduce the chase to its primary constituents (himself, Moby Dick) is to strip from it all vitality, all signs of life. It is quite clear, at least to Ahab, that Starbuck's truncation of his purpose would transform at the most fundamental level the nature of the captain's investigation.

Taken together, Ahab's sense that *knowing the whale is a communal activity* and that *this knowledge is only accountable if it is assembled by the community to which it belongs* constitutes an assault on all arguments that approve the feasibility of "private language." Ahab's attack on the whale, crew in hand, constitutes an attack on Starbuck's sense that "meaning" is something private, clandestine—inside the mind of an individual and not at large in his culture. For Ahab, "meaning" is something that depends on, not what is spoiled by, other people. The target of Ahab's interest, the recipient of his aggression, is the notion that the objects of his immediate experience are the private, shadowy entities that empiricists call sense data. *His* whale is public, influential, real. It could be said of his method that his aim is to change the aspect under which first-person reports of phenomena are understood; his conclusion, that there is no sense to be made of the human condition if the objects of our interest are seen as derivative or unequal to the conceptual structure that invests them with value. According to Ahab, both psychological states and their objects should be seen as equal and reciprocal partners.

This mutuality means, for the fishery, that one's identification of a whale and the properties under which a whale assumes these identifications must be interdependent. This is *not* the case in any system in which a man and his hated fish are separate entities, free to experiment on each other. Starbuck's controlled setup of how to hunt whales—or know what they mean—is a willed activity generally, if not endlessly, repeatable. Its results may be reproduced. Its methodology widely distributed. It takes place in vitro, outside rather than inside a living system. The outcome of this approach is the reduction of a physical existence (like a whale), with all its richness of detail, to conceptual schemata. It splits living reality into elementary components in order to represent the wealth of concrete objects through abstract illustrations which lose the properties of the phenomena themselves. It is addicted to the conventional narrative, where every experience—no matter how knotty or enigmatic—must find its place in the standard storyboard. It depends on an enthusiasm for abstract analysis, regardless of context, in which the reality of human conscious activity is replaced by more mechanical models.

Starbuck identifies the individual with the empty choosing will and the curious liberty of turning one's back on the facts. Freedom, according to Starbuck's model, consists of the sudden leaping of the isolated will in and out of an impersonal logical complex. This is not, however, the way in which perception works. Ahab recognizes that one is likely to identify the moment of choice with the free and empty will only if the *prior* work of attention is ignored. As Iris Murdoch observes in *The Sovereignty of Good,* the task of attention "goes on all the time and at apparently empty and everyday moments we are 'looking,' making those little peering efforts of imagination which have such important cumulative results." (Which is why it is not surprising that Ahab insists how at crucial moments of choice the business of choosing is already over.) Murdoch's model of how perception works, well known to the fishery, "does not imply that we are not free, certainly not," only that "the exercise of freedom is a small piecemeal business which goes on all the time and not a grandiose leaping about unimpeded at important moments."

That Ahab enacts a properly discursive pattern of attention, made familiar by the efforts of Henry James, say, or Proust, attests to his literary, moral character; Ahab does not turn on and off to explicitly moral choices but comes to them from inside a particular moral narrative. Ahab's discursive method accentuates the active role of organization in perception. It emphasizes that observation is never merely the pure description of separate facts but is in collaboration with those facts. (Ahab does not just hunt the whale but knows himself hunted and haunted by it.) Ahab's participant model is complex, unique, nonrecurring. In violation of cultivation. In vivo. He draws attention to the fact that an individual makes specific personalized *use* of a concept.

Ahab's method is derived, like Goethe's, from the desire to see an alternative to mechanistic accounts of stimulus-response. In his study of plants, Goethe came to understand morphology, or the science that gives an object its shape and coherence, as a discipline made possible by studying a thing in its natural environment. In Italy, he writes, "instead of being grown in pots or under glass as they are with us, plants are allowed to grow freely in the open fresh air . . . [where] they become more intelligible." This intelligibility does not indicate some secret essence discoverable because the plant is in its natural habitat, but is a discerning quality created through a scientist's association with his substance—an *association* only conceivable in the wild. This human reading is then brought to nature as an estimate of the plant's own possibilities. Goethe's account of what makes an object coherent is a hypothesis shared by Ahab, who also believes that perceptions are the products not of discrete stimuli but of organized gestalten.

Naturally constituted knowledge, or knowledge in its natural habitat, is also of interest when the object under investigation is man. Clifford Geertz, in *Local Knowledge*, has called for what he terms an "outdoor psychology," or the location of human cognitive activity in context. Cognition alfresco, as it were, is not simply influenced by culture but understood as a cultural process. "Outside" does more than refer to the unpredictable, outdoor world independent from the laboratory. It also points to human cognition as a procedure or operation that cannot simply be housed in a particular body but is dependent for its conception and expression on a variety of hosts. Instead of assuming that knowledge is located inside the skin of a distinct individual (or that an individual furnishes "knowledge" as part of his contribution to society), this model understands human cognition to be a dynamic, inconstant process dependent for its organization on groups of individuals. These groups are responsible as a whole for what might be called cognitive structure. In the whaling industry these groups are known as crews. What knowledge Ahab has, even as captain, is not separate or separable from that wider context of which his private contributions are only a part. Thus not only must Ahab's whale be in its natural habitat, but so must Ahab.

Though Ahab favors a direct approach, he intuits the impracticality of reaching out to the perplexity of this thing *whale* without participating in the culture—the "open fresh air"— that makes it intelligible; and this configuration, this wild assemblage, includes "the incompetence of mere un-aided virtue or right-mindedness in Starbuck, the invulnerable jollity of indifference and recklessness in Starbuck, and the pervading mediocrity in Flask." Aye, and the innocence of Pip, the promise and commitment of Queequeg, and the writerly ambitions of Ishmael, as well. "Such a crew, so officered, seemed specially picked and packed by some infernal fatality" to help Ahab to his final romantic object. "The crew, man, the crew!" cries the captain to his wavering first mate. "Are they not one and all with Ahab, in this matter of the whale?"

The most important thing to understand in this matter of the whale is that, like any other thing, a whale exists separately from man but depends on him (the source of its symbolic weight) for coherence. It is not a cetological feature but a human one that makes the whale seem larger than life. *But a man cannot give an object this kind of figurative import on his own.* Symbol making is a group process; it does not take place "inside" an individual but "outside," or rather, inside a shifting community of individuals. According to Ahab, men don't happen upon whales; whales *happen to them,* which is to say, as Ahab does, that Moby Dick is out in the world, cruising, circulating, before he is on Ahab's mind, or under his skin. Because meaning-making activity does not go on under wraps or inside the body of any one individual but is at large in the community, knowing a thing's meaning is a communal enterprise.

Although he is not known for his cultural sensitivity, if we are too quick to dismiss Ahab or call his pursuit maniacal, we poorly comprehend the insight he makes available. Surrounding the melodrama of the capture—the playing out of man's sublime attachment to the vast body of the leviathan—is another kind of leviathan, a vast, extraordinarily elaborate and detailed body of rules, a culture or form of life whose elasticity the first kind of leviathan depends on for its unity. The whale is an entangled object, wrapped up as it is in the lives and lines of men. Thus Ahab isn't mad or maniacal when he insists that Moby Dick is not the private emblem of his own cognitive performance. What is maddening is Starbuck's model of human knowledge as abstract symbol manipulation, a model that promotes the general belief that meaning exists inside the minds of individuals. *This mistake has consequences,* not the least of which is gradual erosion of the belief that from any one position we can know what one another means.

In *Moby Dick* the objects of our special interests take on a distinctive physiognomy, so that we may interpret them, group ourselves round these objects, and engage each other over them. Regarding particular things in particular ways is what brings them near to us—what marks them out and makes them conspicuous, coordinates man's efforts with his abilities, and offers consolation by imposing design upon what might under different conditions seem intolerably chancy and inconstant. This particular regard for things—a better term, for our purpose, than "obsession"—is the adhesive quality that affords coherence to what is otherwise slippery and oleaginous employment. And this, of course, is the whaling industry's contribution to philosophy: the admonition not to lose sight of a reality separate from ourselves (or to remember those objects that inhabited the earth long before man and will inevitably survive him), and not to undervalue our ability to make sense of such things, our genius for knowing what they mean.

We should, finally, be grateful for the Captain's unrepentant conviction that dissimilar individuals can dispense with a whale in meaningful ways—if only because, as Ahab intuits, a man alone ain't got no bloody chance.

NOTES

I have tried to write a thoughtful book, though of course most of the thoughts that interest me come from other, better books. To these works I am under a certain obligation, but to adopt the posture of the conventional citation in regards to them feels shabby—as if I had attempted to accurately reproduce the arguments of these admired authors; as if I didn't frequently use their choice phrases to strange effect. (My debts are tremendous, but I think badly repaid by the usual formal treatment.) For the volume in hand there are only two books I claim to have read well—by which I mean got involved with intimately on what feels like their terms—Melville's *Moby Dick* and Wittgenstein's *Philosophical Investigations*. Even so, I am not producing an account of these texts so much as adopting the style of their approach, the kind of "advance" on a subject in which the subject is never treated in isolation from the system or culture that gives it meaning. (In which, therefore, one is unable to come upon the subject fresh, in secret, or outside the relationship that made the recognition of it possible.) Thus I am aware this work bears little resemblance to what is traditionally known as literary criticism. My relationship to the material is troublesome because I attempt to understand it both in the light of love and in the light of justice—a difficult activity, as Niels Bohr has said.

The awkward thing here is to explain the indebtedness and the latitude, as regards one's stimuli. I hoped to pursue my subject without explicitly pointing to it, as if it were the *cause* of my interest, and also without expressly pointing away (as if I didn't doggedly believe the subject itself was what drew me). The motivating thing for this kind of pursuit doesn't loiter, enticingly, before one—nor does it lurk in the background; these kinds of chases are not propelled any more than they are provoked. It is in the air, as it were, or more appropriately in the water, a kind of unaccountable but deeply provocative force. (It was for this reason that I soon lost interest in any attempt to measure or otherwise account for Ahab's grossly hypertrophied investment in Moby Dick. The captain's maddening impetus lay neither before him in the shape of a fish nor behind him in the form of a history.) In the following notes, I try to pay some tribute to what colored the waters, long before I entered them. Accordingly the following documentation is not intended to guide readers in a particular direction so much as locate them in the right sea.

INTRODUCING THE SUBJECT (CHAPTER 1)

Owing to its nature, the first chapter is most strikingly in need of documentary support. The brief sampling of Western philosophy is based in part on a casual exploration of some primary texts, particularly Descartes's *Meditations;* Hobbes's *Leviathan;* Locke's *An Essay concerning Human Understanding;* Berkeley's *Principles of Human Knowledge;* Hume's *An Enquiry concerning Human Understanding;* and Kant's *Critique of Pure Reason* and *Critique of Judgement.* I do not wish to feign any wider scholarly background in this area than the average interested reader. Henri Bergson's stage metaphor can be found in *Matter and Memory* (New York: Zone Books, 1991), 14. I owe much to Bergson's insistence on the presence of the body in perception and find him the most eloquent of all the philosophers who say "no psychology without biology," or who participate in what is sometimes called the physiological reinterpretation of Kant's critique of reason. See also Henri Bergson, *Creative Evolution* (Mineola: Dover Publications, 1998). This project is continued in Iris Murdoch's elegant reading of mental concepts as moral concepts, *The Sovereignty of Good* (London: Routledge, 1970).

When I needed a larger view of these philosophical goings-on, I turned to Terry Eagleton's invaluable history and critique of the concept of the aesthetic, *The Ideology of the Aesthetic* (Oxford: Basil Blackwell, 1990). On the constitution of the modern "subject" I was also greatly aided by the work of Henry Sussman—see especially *The Aesthetic Contract* (Stanford: Stanford University Press, 1997).

An early independent study with Professor Sussman ensured my fascination with the topic. Elizabeth Grosz's questions about the body politic ("What kind of genitals are they?") come from her investigation into how the functioning of bodies transforms our understanding of space, time, knowledge, and desire in *Space, Time, and Perversion* (New York: Routledge, 1995). Also having spent some time as her student, I owe much to Grosz's intellectual generosity and emotionally charged, finely crafted philosophical insights (for instance, my brief reading of *The Origin of Species* in chapter 2 was written with her circumspect voice in my head).

My understanding of how the constituting subject plays out in America is due in large part to the work of Franklin, Emerson, and Thoreau: also Thoreau's reading of Emerson, Stanley Cavell's reading of Emerson and Thoreau, and Ken Dauber's reading of Emerson and Franklin. It is difficult to read these writers (or American literature in general) without confronting and coming to terms with the idea that America is constituted along democratic, poetic lines. In other words, America makes meaning as it makes itself, or rather America makes the making of itself the meaningful thing. These ideas are best expressed in Kenneth Dauber's unrivaled *The Idea of Authorship in America: Democratic Poetics from Franklin to Melville* (Madison: University of Wisconsin Press, 1990). This innate American inability to separate form and content should confirm my poetic leanings even while making evident why I do not feel the need to flee the confines of ordinary prose. Speaking of such a departure, however, the comments on subjective prejudice—"Subjective prejudice, in other words, is not what keeps the world at a distance but what ensures its nearness"—are meant to express a kind of ethical poetic grounding and have been formulated with some help from, in particular, Charles Bernstein's explication of what he calls the "poetics of nearness": "In the poetics of nearness, others exist prior to oneself; you do not look out onto other people as if through a preexisting subjectivity, but find whoever you may be as a person, as poet, in relation to them, by virtue of your acknowledgment of their suffering, which is to say their circumstance or bearing in the world" (Charles Bernstein, *My Way* [Chicago: University of Chicago Press, 1999], 217). The curious Bernstein influence should also be clear in chapter 2. (If I do not sound grateful for this influence, I am misrepresenting its importance to me.)

Regarding particular allusions, the quote from Otto Neurath comes from his 1913 paper "The Lost Wanderers of Descartes and the Auxiliary Motive (On the Psychology of Decision)" given to the Vienna Circle. The quote from Karl Popper is from *The Logic of Scientific Discovery* (New York: Basic Books, 1959), 111. The remark about marrying the speech of strangers is summoned from a line of Charles Reznikoff's: "I have married and married the speech of strangers" from *Jerusalem the Golden*, #1, 1:107. The vast bulk of my quotations in this chapter and in those that follow, however, come from two books: Ludwig Wittgenstein, *Philosophical Investigations*, trans. G. E. M. Anscombe (Basil Blackwell and Mott, 1958); and Herman Melville, *Moby Dick*, ed. Harrison Hayford and Hershel Parker (New York: W. W. Norton, 1967). I quote copiously from these works by Wittgenstein and Melville, and although I chose not to litter the page with exegesis, I tried to be honest and unsparing in my collection of evidence. I have no special allegiance to these particular editions.

ANTHROPOLOGY, POETRY, AND THE PACIFIC (CHAPTERS 2 AND 5)

As noted, I am not trying to produce an account of *Moby Dick* so much as adopt the style of its approach—the exploration of a subject in which the subject is never treated in isolation from the system or culture that gives it meaning. This style is one that might be called "anthropological," and some people not officially part of that profession (Wittgenstein, for instance) have referred to their work in such terms. Of course, here it is a good idea to begin with the experts.

Pacific anthropologist Greg Dening's brilliant combination of interpretive anthropology and an exploration of the theatrical nature of shipboard life in *Mr. Bligh's Bad Language* (Cambridge: Cambridge University Press, 1992) was the first *ethical* study of a voyage I had read—by which I mean the first voyage narrative that makes readerly participation explicit. (Only when readers' participation is explicit are readers forced to acknowledge the various ways in which meaning happens, in which we are acting on language as language is acting on us, making meaning while thinking about how meaning gets made. This call on the reader and the reader's inevitable response creates the condition for a readerly ethics. My sense that attention to this condition underwrote Dening's project was one reason why his work has such considerable influence here.) Dening's sense that Captain Bligh misunderstood the theatrical nature of shipboard life, particularly his role as captain, planted the seed of what I now understand to be one of my arguments regarding Ahab. Bligh thought he was being conscientious when he verbally humiliated disobedient sailors instead of subjecting them to corporal punishment—or, for instance, when he forbade dangerous practices such as ducking under the illusion that he was sparing his men some discomfort. His *consideration* for the men, if you could call it that, sought to protect them from something (perhaps themselves). To the men, however, this "protection" served to exclude them from the very practices that established their power and authority. By assuming the weight of their responsibility to him, each other, and their own good health, Bligh cut them out of the loop (and in return they excised the source of their unease). In this sense Ahab's unwillingness to exclude his men, to protect them from himself or themselves, is, strangely, better moral practice than Bligh's. There was little chance of mutiny on the *Pequod,* as Ahab never undermined the men's sense of their influence and participation. On a final note, the conversation about "crossing the Line" owes much to Dening, though in this chapter I also mean to invoke Stanley Cavell's version. (On Cavell's influence, see the final section of notes, "Moral Philosophy and Moral Perfectionism.")

Dening's project follows that of Clifford Geertz. Geertz's basic insistence that "the humanities are connected to its arguments not in the fashion of skeptical bystanders but, as the source of its imagery, chargeable accomplices" is clearly a founding assumption of *Whale!* Geertz's persistent and indefatigable reminder to his readers that "things are what you make of them" (or, as Joseph Butler puts it, "everything is what it is and not another thing") is the premise from which I invariably begin. See Clifford Geertz, *Local Knowledge: Further Essays in Interpretive Anthropology* (New York: Basic Books, 1983), 26, 76. A more recent use of Geertzian "outdoor psychology" (although I would guess Goethe has some prior claim) can be found in Edwin Hutchins, *Cognition in the Wild* (Cambridge: MIT Press, 2000). An anthropologist and ocean-racing sailor, Hutchins grounds his account of cognitive theory in an extended analysis of ship navigation. He does so to emphasize that symbol processing takes place not "inside" the individual but "outside," or rather inside a shifting *community* of groups of individuals. As he says, "symbols are in the world first, and only later in the head" (370). A similar point is made by Miguel Tamen, who also practices a kind of interpretive anthropology in his remarkable *Friends of Interpretable Objects* (Cambridge: Harvard University Press, 2001). Tamen's claim is that an object becomes interpretable only in the context of a "society of friends," from which follows his sense that "there are no interpretable objects or intentional objects, only what counts as an interpretable object or, better, groups of people for whom certain objects count as interpretable and who, accordingly, deal with certain objects in recognizable ways" (3). I was introduced to Professor Tamen's work after this project was on its way to press, but I am hopeful that my business with Ahab and his whale might be seen to play out Tamen's lucid thesis.

Poetic sources were just as vital to *Whale!* as anthropological ones. My sense that whaling and quantum mechanics share the same methodology, or that following the transformation of atomic to subatomic theory sounds a lot like a whale hunt, is indebted for its fleeting vision of the history of science to Stephen Toulmin and June Goodfield's remarkable *The Architecture of Matter* (Chicago: University of Chicago Press, 1962), from which much of the background for chapter 2 comes.

Rumor has it that George Duyckinck's cryptic remark regarding Long Ghost's advice to Melville might be found in a letter to Joann Miller (New York, 23 September 1850, Papers of the Duyckinck family, New York Public Library). The Emerson quotations come from my traveling paperback copy of the *Selected Writings of Emerson*, ed. Donald McQuade (New York: Random House, 1981). The Robert Creeley quote comes from *The Collected Poems of Robert Creeley, 1945–1975* (Berkeley: University of California Press, 1982). For Jack Spicer on "low ghosts" and "vertigo," see *The House That Jack Built: The Collected Lectures of Jack Spicer* (Hanover, N.H.: Wesleyan University Press, 1998). I must thank both Robert Creeley and Susan Howe for giving me a poet's introduction to the work of Spicer, Dickinson, and other American versifiers and in general for entangling my study of American literature with poetic insight. The poet referenced in the preface is Bill Manhire, New Zealand's inaugural poet laureate. The original line reads, "Scientists can seem like embarrassing, marginal figures (almost like poets) in the new corporate New Zealand" (*Doubtful Sounds: Essays and Interviews*

[Victoria: Victoria University Press, 2000], 244). Bill and his wife Marion Mcleod are those kind of book and conversation lovers who model how to live well—if one is lucky enough to enter briefly and awkwardly into their daily activities.

New Zealand poet/curator Ian Wedde's reading of Long Ghost and of Melville's stay in the Pacific is the best I know and adds weight to the contention that poets do it better. What makes this performance even more anomalous is that the remarkable passages quoted here concerning the Ghost and a young Herman Melville form only a small part of *Symmes Hole* (London: Faber and Faber, 1986), the rest of which has to do, in part, with the history of shore-based whaling in nineteenth-century New Zealand, the ugly sexy story of Pacific exploration and the mapping of a "New World" imagination, the role of "failure" and the existence of a history other than the dominant one, ruthless corporatizing, the fate of literati in the Pacific, history that sounds fictional, and paranoia that turns out to be right. I used sizable passages here because *Symmes Hole* is absurdly out of print and hard to find in America. This work makes plain the impossibility of lumping Melville with the "New England" authors instead of rightfully locating him in the less-orthodox Pacific.

My sense of the Pacific owes much to the scholarship of Marshall Sahlins, Greg Dening, T. Walter Herbert Jr., Neil Rennie, Nicholas Thomas, Jonathan Lamb, Bridget Orr, Vanessa Smith, Paul Lyons, Pat Hohepa, Rod Edmund, Murray Edmund, Mark Houlahan, Stephen Turner, Epeli Hau'ofa, Rob Wilson, and, in particular, Alex Calder. For chapter 5 see especially *Voyages and Beaches: Pacific Encounters, 1769–1840*, ed. Alex Calder, Jonathan Lamb, and Bridget Orr (Honolulu: University of Hawai'i Press, 1999).

ON DISCURSIVE PRACTICE (CHAPTERS 3 AND 4)

I have been greatly aided in my reading of Wittgenstein by Ray Monk's revelatory *Ludwig Wittgenstein: The Duty of Genius* (New York: Penguin Books, 1990). Monk's philosophical autobiography is filled with remarks that I found indispensable for a proper engagement with Ahab and Melville. For instance, when Wittgenstein believed that he would not finish a polished, published copy of *Philosophical Investigations* before his death but still wanted his friends to read and understand it, he "considered having it mimeographed and distributed among his friends with expressions of dissatisfaction, like: 'This is not quite right' or: *'This is fishy,'* written in parentheses after remarks that needed revision" (555; italics mine).

Wittgenstein was always interested in the medical profession, and the prevalence of discursive lines of thought among psychologists, psychiatrists, and neurologists should come as no surprise. My use of the term "pathological" to describe that which is not understood discursively stems in part from a reading of Grant Gillet's fascinating *The Mind and Its Discontents: An Essay in Discursive Psychiatry* (Oxford: Oxford University Press). Here a pathological psychiatric project is one that finds the isolation of a recognizable malfunction an appropriate system for studying and trying to correct it. Gillet is a practicing neurosurgeon with additional qualifications in psychiatry who completed a D.Phil. in philosophy at Oxford. His Wittgensteinian arguments have considerable implications for the way in which people suffering from psychiatric disorders are treated and understood.

I believe a necessary source for understanding Wittgenstein is the late "romantic" work of the great Russian neuropsychologist A. R. Luria. Reading *The Man with a Shattered World* (Cambridge: Harvard University Press, 1972) makes it possible to understand what Wittgenstein meant by "having a grammar"—not because Luria specifically refers to Wittgenstein but because this case study shows with care and in detail what it's like *not* to have a grammar, thus making it clearer what having one could possibly mean. See also A. R. Luria, *The Mind of a Mnemonist* (Cambridge: Harvard University Press, 1968).

In 1924 Luria attended a talk by the twenty-eight-year-old Lev Vygotsky, who was challenging the leading Soviet behavioral scientists by arguing that psychology could not ignore the fact of consciousness. Described by Alex Kozulin as a "strange transplant from the era of encyclopedists and romantics to the age of commissars and conditional reflexes," Vygotsky was an early critic of atomistic modes of analysis. I am particularly interested in Vygotsky's sense that "decomposition shows only the material with which the higher functions are built, but says nothing about their construction," and thus we are often "looking in the wrong directions" when we allow ourselves to think about meaning as an inalienable part of the word itself. See Lev Vygotsky, *Thought and Language* (Cambridge: MIT Press, 1986). It was from this work that I especially learned to distrust theory based on the sign as a means of communication. Communication requires a mediating system, which means, as Vygotsky puts it, that any kind of reference "already requires generalization"—which I take to be another way of saying, with Wittgenstein, that language requires agreement not just in definitions but in judgments.

Vygotsky also had a keen interest in William James's *The Varieties of Religious Experience,* which further points to Vygotsky's preoccupation with specifically *human* purpose and capacity. The lines from William James in chapter 4 are taken from *Pragmatism and Other Writings* (New York: Penguin Books, 2000), particularly Lecture IV, "The Will to Believe," and "The Moral Philosopher and the Moral Life." For Richard Rorty on intellectual responsibility, see, for example, *Consequences of Pragmatism* (Minneapolis: University of Minnesota Press, 1982), or *Objectivity, Relativism, and Truth: Philosophical Papers I* (Cambridge: Cambridge University Press, 1991). My sense that today's pragmatism is not at all James's pragmatism (and sometimes that James's pragmatism was not James's pragmatism) comes from the feeling that what has largely been cut from the Jamesian version is his account of belief. Belief, somewhat of an embarrassment to the neopragmatists, has been replaced with a more secular political agenda. Because I think exorcising belief from pragmatism guts the entire project, my distrust of the replacement should be clear.

MORAL PHILOSOPHY AND MORAL PERFECTIONISM (CHAPTERS 4, 6, AND CONCLUSION)

I am only a novice in the area of moral philosophy, but I find this field's matter and discourse of paramount interest. If I did not know when I began that this was a conversation I was trying to enter, I do now. (Wittgenstein has been accused in various ways of exempting himself from moral philosophy, but I hope to show here how much his sympathies are in keeping, in "queer ways," with those of, say, Simone Weil, Iris Murdoch, Cora Diamond, David Wiggins, and Martha Nussbaum.) In particular and in reference to chapter 4, the idea that relativity is in itself no obstacle to certainty is best expressed in David Wiggins's incomparable collection of work on the philosophy of value, *Needs, Values, Truth*

(Oxford: Oxford University Press, 1987). I cannot properly express how much intelligence is contained in this volume. It is Wiggins who maintains that an adequate account of the human condition will have to "treat psychological states and their objects as equal and reciprocal partners" (106), a founding postulate of *Whale!*

Ahab's sense that those people with whom you share a history are the very folks who can leave you shipwrecked and drowning is brought to life in Salman Rushdie's recent novels *The Ground beneath Her Feet* and *Fury*. I find it encouraging that as good and careful a man as Rushdie might see Ahab's point here.

My belief that equating Ahab's violence toward the whale with groundless hostility allows readers to dismiss his desperation and intent was picked up from Stanley Cavell's reading of the ancient mariner in *In Quest of the Ordinary: Lines of Skepticism and Romanticism* (Chicago: University of Chicago Press, 1988), 56. I'm not sure how to document the influence of Cavell's work on a book like *Whale!* except to say my introduction to Cavell (through the library, of course) signaled the end of one life and the beginning of another. His influence should be felt, therefore, at every turn and at each possible point of interest. See particularly *The Claim of Reason: Wittgenstein, Skepticism, Morality, and Tragedy* (Oxford: Oxford University Press, 1979); *The Senses of Walden* (Chicago: University of Chicago Press, 1972); *Conditions Handsome and Unhandsome: The Constitution of Emersonian Perfectionism* (Chicago: University of Chicago Press, 1990); and *This New Yet Unapproachable America: Lectures after Emerson after Wittgenstein* (Albuquerque: Living Batch Press, 1989).

ACKNOWLEDGMENTS

I wrote the bulk of this book while on a Fulbright fellowship to New Zealand in 1999 and 2000, which gave me time to think about how I found myself in the middle of the Pacific, and how Ahab found himself there, and for which I am very grateful. An NEH summer seminar on ethics and aesthetics at the University of North Carolina, Chapel Hill, directed by John McGowan and Allen Dunn, greatly improved its moral character. At SUNY Buffalo and to my inestimable advantage I encountered my mentor Kenneth Dauber, and it is to Ken's question, casually put ("What if *Moby Dick* isn't a book about a whale, but a whale of a book?"), that I have been attempting to respond; if the response is any good, it is principally a measure of this man and the quality of his questions.

I was pushing a project, a rude, rough-cut kind of literary criticism that encouraged an "unhealthy" proximity to its subject, and for this I needed both approval and discipline. A whole company of relations had the grace to grant me an allowance and the wit to push back, in particular my generous parents (to whom I am greatly indebted for early outfitting and routine refurbishment), Lorna and Shel Hershinow, Luanna Meyer, and Ian Evans. Also my extended family of cronies and confidantes: especially the Hoffmans and 84 Hodge, clan librarian Jane Evans, the guests and host of Beth Stover's annual Moby Dick parties, the Bellingham beauties, my boxing coach, a dramaturge, the New Plymouth contingent (special aroha to S. Kaan), and, in the early years, the formidably patient Sir Wade. I am grateful to initial readers Charles Bernstein, Alex Calder, Liz Grosz, and Henry Sussman, as well as the author of a remarkably generous reader's report, Cesare Casarino. Cheers to Douglas Armato and the University of Minnesota Press for giving me a chance. Hats off to the talented Tom Wood. In the final stages of the project, I found myself among new colleagues at the University of Redlands, and I remain overwhelmed by their grace and good humor. For their steady affection: Sarah and Andrew, Sam and Bri, Joni and Douglas, Melany and Keith, the Bernsteins, Jenna, Adam, Gia, Ian, Jamesa, Bridgie, Kathy Ray, and my wonderful brother David. For his courage, Dallas. Most particularly I would like to thank Beth Dill and Joel Bettridge, who never got out of the boat.

K. L. EVANS is assistant professor of English at the University of Redlands in California.